C#.NET SOURCE CODE: MANAGEMENT OBJECT SEARCHER

Richard Edwards

INTRODUCTION

A long time ago, I made a commitment to learn how to play a game called Drakes Uncharted Fortune. It was, at the time, a first-person shooter and I learned how to play it rather well. My problem is when I devote a lot of my off time to such moments of trivial sweetness, I also expect the people who said there would be a lot more to come over the years, to decide not to continue it. I fully expected it to outlast me and I would be seen in a coffin with game controller in my hand playing the latest game to completion. I just wouldn't know I hadn't.

Sadly, "A Thief's End" put an end to that dream. And, believe it or not, I refused to play that last game for almost 2 years after it came out because I really never wanted to let go of the main characters.

Especially, Scully.

For me, they became family.

This book was written with one thing in mind. Provide you with code that you learn from and work with. In fact, I consider this book to be something you can collect and work with over the course of your entire IT career.

Most books are, by nature, are written by subject experts who are very good at what they do. Very few are written by real programmers.

Programmers are the druids of computer programming. They tend to be soft spoken and easy going. Very focused and not wandering far from the computer keyboard.

I am neither one.

I am a writer who has been a programmer, developer and a solution expert for over the past 30 years. And as such, I am wanting to share my work with you in a rather unique way.

The book was written around the work contained in one class that from top to bottom comes out to 1850 lines of tested and reusable code. It was written in roughly 2 hours and it will take me the better part of a day for me to explain what each routine does and how you can make the routine more robust.

I can't do all of the work for you. Your own personal touch can go a long- ways.

There are also 10 pages of code which will help you create a physical overview of all namespaces and classes that is currently on your dev box. Beyond that, the rest of the work in this book is designed to be called by a form with the intent to produce reusable code.

Unfortunately, many of the routines in this book are also dedicated in that they must be used by the Win32_Process. But you can and should be able to see where changing the word Process to Bios, ComputerSystem, Product, or over 700 other names can easily turn the routines into something else entirely different.

WHAT WMI NAMESPACES AND CLASSES ARE ON YOUR MACHINE?

Someone once said, "It is what you don't know that can kill you," Well, they might not have said it exactly that way, but you get the idea.

How can you use something that exists on your machine, but you don't know it?

Back in 2002, I created something called the WMI Explorer. Microsoft came out with their version in May of 2003. Neither one of us cared, It pretty much fell flat on its face.

The biggest difference between the two is my class groupings was based on the way the classes were presented. In-other-words, I there was no underscore, the category was the classname. If there was an underscore at the beginning of the classname, it was a superclass. It there was an underscore in the middle of the classname, the letters before the underscore became its category.

I thought it was a pretty good idea at the time.

Apparently, no one else did. Fact is, the concept was never used by anyone else and WMI Explorer that other people began to "create" used the Microsoft template and never did consider a more granular approach.

I also think the other reason why the WMI Explorer didn't become popular was because of the lack of documentation beyond the most common root: root\cimv2. And back in 2003 time, there were less than a few hundred of them.

But today is a completely different ballpark. Today there are literally hundreds of classes under root\cimv2 alone.

Would you like your own personal copy?

The following scripts that I've been using since 2002, will make that happen for you. Just create a folder on your desktop, then copy and paste the three scripts into that directory and start with namespaces.vbs and end with classes.vbs.

NAMESPACES.VBS

```
Dim fso
Dim l
Dim s


EnumNamespaces("root")

Sub EnumNamespaces(ByVal nspace)

Set ws = CreateObject("Wscript.Shell")
Set fso = CreateObject("Scripting.FilesystemObject")

If fso.folderExists(ws.currentDirectory & "\" & nspace) = false then
fso.CreateFolder(ws.currentDirectory & "\" & nspace)
End If

On error Resume Next

Set          objs          =          GetObject("Winmgmts:\\.\"          &
nspace).InstancesOf("__Namespace", &H20000)

If err.Number <> 0 Then
err.Clear
Exit Sub
End If

For each obj in objs
```

```
    EnumNamespaces(nspace & "\" & obj.Name)
    Next

    End Sub
```

Categories.VBS

```
  Dim fso
  Dim l
  Dim s

  Set ws = CreateObject("Wscript.Shell")
  Set fso = CreateObject("Scripting.FilesystemObject")

  EnumNamespaces("root")


  Sub EnumNamespaces(ByVal nspace)

  EnumCategories(nspace)

  If fso.folderExists(ws.currentDirectory & "\" & nspace) = false then
  fso.CreateFolder(ws.currentDirectory & "\" & nspace)
  End If

  On error Resume Next

  Set      objs      =       GetObject("Winmgmts:\\.\"        &
nspace).InstancesOf("___Namespace", &H20000)

    If err.Number <> 0 Then
    err.Clear
    Exit Sub
```

```
End If

For each obj in objs

EnumNamespaces(nspace & "\" & obj.Name)

Next

End Sub

Sub EnumCategories(ByVal nspace)

Set ws = CreateObject("Wscript.Shell")
Set fso = CreateObject("Scripting.FilesystemObject")

Set objs = GetObject("Winmgmts:\\.\" & nspace).SubClassesOf("", &H20000)
For each obj in objs

pos = instr(obj.Path_.class, "_")

if pos = 0 then
If fso.folderExists(ws.currentDirectory & "\" & nspace & "\" & obj.Path_.Class)
= false then
fso.CreateFolder(ws.currentDirectory & "\" & nspace & "\" & obj.Path_.Class)
End If
else
if pos = 1 then
If fso.folderExists(ws.currentDirectory & "\" & nspace & "\SuperClasses") =
false then
fso.CreateFolder(ws.currentDirectory & "\" & nspace & "\SuperClasses")
End If
else
```

```
      If   fso.folderExists(ws.currentDirectory   &   "\"   &   nspace   &   "\"   &
Mid(obj.Path_.Class, 1, pos-1)) = false then
      fso.CreateFolder(ws.currentDirectory   &   "\"   &   nspace   &   "\"   &
Mid(obj.Path_.Class, 1, pos-1))
      End If
      End If
      End If


      Next


      End Sub
```

Classes.VBS

```
      Dim fso
      Dim l
      Dim s

      EnumNamespaces("root")

      Sub EnumNamespaces(ByVal nspace)

      EnumClasses(nspace)

      Set ws = CreateObject("Wscript.Shell")
      Set fso = CreateObject("Scripting.FilesystemObject")

      If fso.folderExists(ws.currentDirectory & "\" & nspace) = false then
      fso.CreateFolder(ws.currentDirectory & "\" & nspace)
      End If

      On error Resume Next
```

```
Set        objs        =        GetObject("Winmgmts:\\.\"        &
nspace).InstancesOf("___Namespace", &H20000)

If err.Number <> 0 Then
err.Clear
Exit Sub
End If

For each obj in objs

EnumNamespaces(nspace & "\" & obj.Name)

Next

End Sub

Sub EnumClasses(ByVal nspace)

Set ws = CreateObject("Wscript.Shell")
Set fso = CreateObject("Scripting.FilesystemObject")

Set objs = GetObject("Winmgmts:\\.\" & nspace).SubClassesOf("", &H20000)
For each obj in objs

pos = instr(obj.Path_.class, "_")

if pos = 0 then
    call   CreateXMLFile(ws.CurrentDirectory   &   "\"   &   nspace   &   "\"   &
obj.Path_.Class, nspace, obj.Path_.Class)
    else
    if pos = 1 then
```

```
        call  CreateXMlFile(ws.CurrentDirectory  &  "\"  &  nspace  &  "\Superclasses",
nspace, obj.Path_.Class)
        else
        call    CreateXMLFile(ws.CurrentDirectory    &    "\"    &    nspace    &    "\"    &
Mid(obj.Path_.Class, 1, pos-1), nspace, obj.Path_.Class)
        End If
        End If


        Next


        End Sub


        Sub CreateXMLFile(ByVal Path, ByVal nspace, ByVal ClassName)



        Set fso = CreateObject("Scripting.FileSystemObject")
        Dim shorty
        On error Resume Next
        shorty = fso.GetFolder(Path).ShortPath
        If err.Number <> 0 then
        err.Clear
        Exit Sub
        End IF



        set obj = GetObject("Winmgmts:\\.\" & nspace).Get(classname)

        Set txtstream = fso.OpenTextFile(Shorty & "\" & Classname & ".xml", 2, true, -
2)
        txtstream.WriteLine("<data>")
        txtstream.WriteLine(" <NamespaceInformation>")
        txtstream.WriteLine("   <namespace>" & nspace & "</namespace>")
```

```
txtstream.WriteLine("    <classname>" & classname & "</classname>")
txtstream.WriteLine("  </NamespaceInformation>")
txtstream.WriteLine("  <properties>")

for each prop in obj.Properties_
txtstream.WriteLine("        <property Name = """ & prop.Name & """
IsArray=""" & prop.IsArray & """ DataType = """ &
prop.Qualifiers_("CIMType").Value & """/>")
Next
txtstream.WriteLine("  </properties>")
txtstream.WriteLine("</data>")
txtstream.close

End sub
```

As shown below, once these routines are done, you should be able to go to the folder, based on what I've told you about the Namespace\category\classes

And If you open one of these up:

```xml
- <data>
  - <NamespaceInformation>
      <namespace>root\CIMV2</namespace>
      <classname>Win32_BIOS</classname>
    </NamespaceInformation>
  - <properties>
      <property Name="BiosCharacteristics" IsArray="True" DataType="uint16"/>
      <property Name="BIOSVersion" IsArray="True" DataType="string"/>
      <property Name="BuildNumber" IsArray="False" DataType="string"/>
      <property Name="Caption" IsArray="False" DataType="string"/>
      <property Name="CodeSet" IsArray="False" DataType="string"/>
      <property Name="CurrentLanguage" IsArray="False" DataType="string"/>
      <property Name="Description" IsArray="False" DataType="string"/>
      <property Name="IdentificationCode" IsArray="False" DataType="string"/>
      <property Name="InstallableLanguages" IsArray="False" DataType="uint16"/>
      <property Name="InstallDate" IsArray="False" DataType="datetime"/>
      <property Name="LanguageEdition" IsArray="False" DataType="string"/>
      <property Name="ListOfLanguages" IsArray="True" DataType="string"/>
      <property Name="Manufacturer" IsArray="False" DataType="string"/>
      <property Name="Name" IsArray="False" DataType="string"/>
      <property Name="OtherTargetOS" IsArray="False" DataType="string"/>
      <property Name="PrimaryBIOS" IsArray="False" DataType="boolean"/>
      <property Name="ReleaseDate" IsArray="False" DataType="datetime"/>
      <property Name="SerialNumber" IsArray="False" DataType="string"/>
      <property Name="SMBIOSBIOSVersion" IsArray="False" DataType="string"/>
      <property Name="SMBIOSMajorVersion" IsArray="False" DataType="uint16"/>
      <property Name="SMBIOSMinorVersion" IsArray="False" DataType="uint16"/>
      <property Name="SMBIOSPresent" IsArray="False" DataType="boolean"/>
      <property Name="SoftwareElementID" IsArray="False" DataType="string"/>
      <property Name="SoftwareElementState" IsArray="False" DataType="uint16"/>
      <property Name="Status" IsArray="False" DataType="string"/>
      <property Name="TargetOperatingSystem" IsArray="False" DataType="uint16"/>
      <property Name="Version" IsArray="False" DataType="string"/>
    </properties>
  </data>
```

GETTING STARTED

Whether you are using Visual Studio 2010 or higher, the first thing you're going to want to do is create a new Windows Application project in C#.Net. The second thing you're going to need to do is make a few references:

From the list of .Net namespaces:

ADODB

Microsoft.Office.Interop.Excel

System.Management

From the list of .COM namespaces:

Microsoft Scripting Runtime

Microsoft Shell Controls and Automation

```csharp
using System;
using System.Collections.Generic;
using System.Linq;
using System.Text;
using System.Management;
using ADODB;
using Scripting;
using Shell32;
using Microsoft.Office.Interop;
namespace WindowsFormsApplication5
{
    class Class2
    {
```

DECLARING VARIABLES

As you can see from the below code, we are enabling the use of specific variables and objects at the very top of the module ns is made public so that the form can specify what WMI namespace will be used by the program along with what class will be called upon to provide us with information about your local machine. The old school version of the FileSystem Object is created along with an empty object we're going to be using as the textstream.

```
Dictionary<Int32, string> Names = new Dictionary<Int32, string>();
Dictionary<Int32, Dictionary<Int32, string>> Rows = new Dictionary<Int32, Dictionary<Int32, string>>();
String Orientation = "Multi-Line Horizontal";
String Delim = "";
```

INITIALIZATION CODE

The purpose of this function is to return a collection of objects and properties we can use to populate and view in a variety of formats and orientations.

```
public void initialize()
   {
            int x = 0;
            int y = 0;

            ConnectionOptions cops = new ConnectionOptions();
            cops.Authentication =
AuthenticationLevel.PacketPrivacy;
            cops.Impersonation = ImpersonationLevel.Impersonate;
            cops.Locale = "MS_0409";

            ManagementPath path = new ManagementPath();
            path.NamespacePath = "root\\cimv2";
            path.Server = "LocalHost";

            ManagementScope Scope = new ManagementScope(path,
cops);
            Scope.Connect();

            ManagementObjectSearcher mos = new
ManagementObjectSearcher();
            mos.Scope = Scope;
```

```csharp
            mos.Query.QueryString = "Select * from
Win32_Process";
            ManagementObjectCollection moc = mos.Get();
            foreach (ManagementObject mo in moc)
            {
                foreach (PropertyData prop in mo.Properties)
                {
                    Names[x] = prop.Name;
                    x = x + 1;
                }
                x = 0;
                break;
            }

            foreach (ManagementObject mo in moc)
            {
                Dictionary<Int32, string> col = new
Dictionary<Int32, string>();
                foreach (PropertyData prop in mo.Properties)
                {
                    col[x] = GetValue(prop.Name, mo);
                    x = x + 1;
                }
                x = 0;
                Rows[y] = col;
                y = y + 1;

            }

            Create_HTML_Code();

        }
```

CREATE ASP CODE

Inside this sub routine is the code to create an ASP Webpage.

```
private void Create_ASP_Code()
{

    Scripting.FileSystemObject fso = new
Scripting.FileSystemObject();
    Scripting.TextStream txtstream =
fso.OpenTextFile(System.Environment.CurrentDirectory +
"\\Process.asp", Scripting.IOMode.ForWriting, true,
Scripting.Tristate.TristateUseDefault);
    txtstream.WriteLine("<html
xmlns=\"http://www.w3.org/1999/xhtml\">");
    txtstream.WriteLine("<head>");
    txtstream.WriteLine("<title>Win32_Process</title>");
    txtstream.WriteLine("<style type='text/css'>");
    txtstream.WriteLine("body");
    txtstream.WriteLine("{");
    txtstream.WriteLine("    PADDING-RIGHT: 0px;");
    txtstream.WriteLine("    PADDING-LEFT: 0px;");
    txtstream.WriteLine("    PADDING-BOTTOM: 0px;");
    txtstream.WriteLine("    MARGIN: 0px;");
    txtstream.WriteLine("    COLOR: #333;");
    txtstream.WriteLine("    PADDING-TOP: 0px;");
    txtstream.WriteLine("    FONT-FAMILY: verdana, arial,
helvetica, sans-serif;");
    txtstream.WriteLine("}");
    txtstream.WriteLine("table");
    txtstream.WriteLine("{");
    txtstream.WriteLine("    BORDER-RIGHT: #999999 1px
solid;");
```

```
            txtstream.WriteLine("    PADDING-RIGHT: 1px;");
            txtstream.WriteLine("    PADDING-LEFT: 1px;");
            txtstream.WriteLine("    PADDING-BOTTOM: 1px;");
            txtstream.WriteLine("    LINE-HEIGHT: 8px;");
            txtstream.WriteLine("    PADDING-TOP: 1px;");
            txtstream.WriteLine("    BORDER-BOTTOM: #999 1px
solid;");
            txtstream.WriteLine("    BACKGROUND-COLOR:
#eeeeee;");
            txtstream.WriteLine("
filter:progid:DXImageTransform.Microsoft.Shadow(color='silver',
Direction=135, Strength=16)");
            txtstream.WriteLine("}");
            txtstream.WriteLine("th");
            txtstream.WriteLine("{");
            txtstream.WriteLine("    BORDER-RIGHT: #999999 3px
solid;");
            txtstream.WriteLine("    PADDING-RIGHT: 6px;");
            txtstream.WriteLine("    PADDING-LEFT: 6px;");
            txtstream.WriteLine("    FONT-WEIGHT: Bold;");
            txtstream.WriteLine("    FONT-SIZE: 14px;");
            txtstream.WriteLine("    PADDING-BOTTOM: 6px;");
            txtstream.WriteLine("    COLOR: darkred;");
            txtstream.WriteLine("    LINE-HEIGHT: 14px;");
            txtstream.WriteLine("    PADDING-TOP: 6px;");
            txtstream.WriteLine("    BORDER-BOTTOM: #999 1px
solid;");
            txtstream.WriteLine("    BACKGROUND-COLOR:
#eeeeee;");
            txtstream.WriteLine("    FONT-FAMILY: font-family:
Cambria, serif;");
            txtstream.WriteLine("    FONT-SIZE: 12px;");
            txtstream.WriteLine("    text-align: left;");
            txtstream.WriteLine("    white-Space: nowrap;");
            txtstream.WriteLine("}");
            txtstream.WriteLine(".th");
            txtstream.WriteLine("{");
            txtstream.WriteLine("    BORDER-RIGHT: #999999 2px
solid;");
            txtstream.WriteLine("    PADDING-RIGHT: 6px;");
            txtstream.WriteLine("    PADDING-LEFT: 6px;");
            txtstream.WriteLine("    FONT-WEIGHT: Bold;");
            txtstream.WriteLine("    PADDING-BOTTOM: 6px;");
            txtstream.WriteLine("    COLOR: black;");
            txtstream.WriteLine("    PADDING-TOP: 6px;");
```

```
            txtstream.WriteLine("    BORDER-BOTTOM: #999 2px
solid;");
            txtstream.WriteLine("    BACKGROUND-COLOR:
#eeeeee;");
            txtstream.WriteLine("    FONT-FAMILY: font-family:
Cambria, serif;");
            txtstream.WriteLine("    FONT-SIZE: 10px;");
            txtstream.WriteLine("    text-align: right;");
            txtstream.WriteLine("    white-Space: nowrap;");
            txtstream.WriteLine("}");
            txtstream.WriteLine("td");
            txtstream.WriteLine("{");
            txtstream.WriteLine("    BORDER-RIGHT: #999999 3px
solid;");
            txtstream.WriteLine("    PADDING-RIGHT: 6px;");
            txtstream.WriteLine("    PADDING-LEFT: 6px;");
            txtstream.WriteLine("    FONT-WEIGHT: Normal;");
            txtstream.WriteLine("    PADDING-BOTTOM: 6px;");
            txtstream.WriteLine("    COLOR: navy;");
            txtstream.WriteLine("    LINE-HEIGHT: 14px;");
            txtstream.WriteLine("    PADDING-TOP: 6px;");
            txtstream.WriteLine("    BORDER-BOTTOM: #999 1px
solid;");
            txtstream.WriteLine("    BACKGROUND-COLOR:
#eeeeee;");
            txtstream.WriteLine("    FONT-FAMILY: font-family:
Cambria, serif;");
            txtstream.WriteLine("    FONT-SIZE: 12px;");
            txtstream.WriteLine("    text-align: left;");
            txtstream.WriteLine("    white-Space: nowrap;");
            txtstream.WriteLine("}");
            txtstream.WriteLine("div");
            txtstream.WriteLine("{");
            txtstream.WriteLine("    BORDER-RIGHT: #999999 3px
solid;");
            txtstream.WriteLine("    PADDING-RIGHT: 6px;");
            txtstream.WriteLine("    PADDING-LEFT: 6px;");
            txtstream.WriteLine("    FONT-WEIGHT: Normal;");
            txtstream.WriteLine("    PADDING-BOTTOM: 6px;");
            txtstream.WriteLine("    COLOR: white;");
            txtstream.WriteLine("    PADDING-TOP: 6px;");
            txtstream.WriteLine("    BORDER-BOTTOM: #999 1px
solid;");
            txtstream.WriteLine("    BACKGROUND-COLOR: navy;");
```

```
            txtstream.WriteLine("    FONT-FAMILY: font-family:
Cambria, serif;");
            txtstream.WriteLine("    FONT-SIZE: 10px;");
            txtstream.WriteLine("    text-align: left;");
            txtstream.WriteLine("    white-Space: nowrap;");
            txtstream.WriteLine("}");
            txtstream.WriteLine("span");
            txtstream.WriteLine("{");
            txtstream.WriteLine("    BORDER-RIGHT: #999999 3px
solid;");
            txtstream.WriteLine("    PADDING-RIGHT: 3px;");
            txtstream.WriteLine("    PADDING-LEFT: 3px;");
            txtstream.WriteLine("    FONT-WEIGHT: Normal;");
            txtstream.WriteLine("    PADDING-BOTTOM: 3px;");
            txtstream.WriteLine("    COLOR: white;");
            txtstream.WriteLine("    PADDING-TOP: 3px;");
            txtstream.WriteLine("    BORDER-BOTTOM: #999 1px
solid;");
            txtstream.WriteLine("    BACKGROUND-COLOR: navy;");
            txtstream.WriteLine("    FONT-FAMILY: font-family:
Cambria, serif;");
            txtstream.WriteLine("    FONT-SIZE: 10px;");
            txtstream.WriteLine("    text-align: left;");
            txtstream.WriteLine("    white-Space: nowrap;");
            txtstream.WriteLine("    display: inline-block;");
            txtstream.WriteLine("    width: 100%;");
            txtstream.WriteLine("}");
            txtstream.WriteLine("textarea");
            txtstream.WriteLine("{");
            txtstream.WriteLine("    BORDER-RIGHT: #999999 3px
solid;");
            txtstream.WriteLine("    PADDING-RIGHT: 3px;");
            txtstream.WriteLine("    PADDING-LEFT: 3px;");
            txtstream.WriteLine("    FONT-WEIGHT: Normal;");
            txtstream.WriteLine("    PADDING-BOTTOM: 3px;");
            txtstream.WriteLine("    COLOR: white;");
            txtstream.WriteLine("    PADDING-TOP: 3px;");
            txtstream.WriteLine("    BORDER-BOTTOM: #999 1px
solid;");
            txtstream.WriteLine("    BACKGROUND-COLOR: navy;");
            txtstream.WriteLine("    FONT-FAMILY: font-family:
Cambria, serif;");
            txtstream.WriteLine("    FONT-SIZE: 10px;");
            txtstream.WriteLine("    text-align: left;");
            txtstream.WriteLine("    white-Space: nowrap;");
```

```
        txtstream.WriteLine("    width: 100%;");
        txtstream.WriteLine("}");
        txtstream.WriteLine("select");
        txtstream.WriteLine("{");
        txtstream.WriteLine("    BORDER-RIGHT: #999999 3px
solid;");
        txtstream.WriteLine("    PADDING-RIGHT: 6px;");
        txtstream.WriteLine("    PADDING-LEFT: 6px;");
        txtstream.WriteLine("    FONT-WEIGHT: Normal;");
        txtstream.WriteLine("    PADDING-BOTTOM: 6px;");
        txtstream.WriteLine("    COLOR: white;");
        txtstream.WriteLine("    PADDING-TOP: 6px;");
        txtstream.WriteLine("    BORDER-BOTTOM: #999 1px
solid;");
        txtstream.WriteLine("    BACKGROUND-COLOR: navy;");
        txtstream.WriteLine("    FONT-FAMILY: font-family:
Cambria, serif;");
        txtstream.WriteLine("    FONT-SIZE: 10px;");
        txtstream.WriteLine("    text-align: left;");
        txtstream.WriteLine("    white-Space: nowrap;");
        txtstream.WriteLine("    width: 100%;");
        txtstream.WriteLine("}");
        txtstream.WriteLine("input");
        txtstream.WriteLine("{");
        txtstream.WriteLine("    BORDER-RIGHT: #999999 3px
solid;");
        txtstream.WriteLine("    PADDING-RIGHT: 3px;");
        txtstream.WriteLine("    PADDING-LEFT: 3px;");
        txtstream.WriteLine("    FONT-WEIGHT: Bold;");
        txtstream.WriteLine("    PADDING-BOTTOM: 3px;");
        txtstream.WriteLine("    COLOR: white;");
        txtstream.WriteLine("    PADDING-TOP: 3px;");
        txtstream.WriteLine("    BORDER-BOTTOM: #999 1px
solid;");
        txtstream.WriteLine("    BACKGROUND-COLOR: navy;");
        txtstream.WriteLine("    FONT-FAMILY: font-family:
Cambria, serif;");
        txtstream.WriteLine("    FONT-SIZE: 12px;");
        txtstream.WriteLine("    text-align: left;");
        txtstream.WriteLine("    display: table-cell;");
        txtstream.WriteLine("    white-Space: nowrap;");
        txtstream.WriteLine("    width: 100%;");
        txtstream.WriteLine("}");
        txtstream.WriteLine("h1 {");
        txtstream.WriteLine("color: antiquewhite;");
```

```
            txtstream.WriteLine("text-shadow: 1px 1px 1px
black;");
            txtstream.WriteLine("padding: 3px;");
            txtstream.WriteLine("text-align: center;");
            txtstream.WriteLine("box-shadow: inset 2px 2px 5px
rgba(0,0,0,0.5), inset -2px -2px 5px rgba(255,255,255,0.5)");
            txtstream.WriteLine("}");
            txtstream.WriteLine("</style>");
            txtstream.WriteLine("</head>");
            txtstream.WriteLine("<body>");
            txtstream.WriteLine("<%");
            txtstream.WriteLine("Response.Write(\"<table
Border='1' cellpadding='1' cellspacing='1'>\" + vbcrlf)");


            switch (Orientation)
            {


                case "Single-Line Horizontal":
                    {
                        for (int y = 0; y < Rows.Count; y++)
                        {

txtstream.WriteLine("Response.Write(\"<tr>\" + vbcrlf)");
                            for (int x = 0; x < Names.Count; x++)
                            {

txtstream.WriteLine("Response.Write(\"<th>" + Names[x] + "</th>\"
+ vbcrlf)");
                            }

txtstream.WriteLine("Response.Write(\"</tr>\" + vbcrlf)");

txtstream.WriteLine("Response.Write(\"<tr>\" + vbcrlf)");
                            for (int x = 0; x < Names.Count; x++)
                            {
                                String value = Rows[y][x];

txtstream.WriteLine("Response.Write(\"<td>" + value + "</td>\" +
vbcrlf)");
                            }

txtstream.WriteLine("Response.Write(\"</tr>\" + vbcrlf)");
                        break;
```

```
                    }
                    break;
                }
            case "Multi-Line Horizontal":
                {
                    for (int y = 0; y < Rows.Count; y++)
                    {
txtstream.WriteLine("Response.Write(\"<tr>\" + vbcrlf)");
                        for (int x = 0; x < Names.Count; x++)
                        {
txtstream.WriteLine("Response.Write(\"<th>" + Names[x] + "</th>\"
+ vbcrlf)");
                        }
txtstream.WriteLine("Response.Write(\"</tr>\" + vbcrlf)");
                        break;
                    }
                    for (int y = 0; y < Rows.Count; y++)
                    {
txtstream.WriteLine("Response.Write(\"<tr>\" + vbcrlf)");
                        for (int x = 0; x < Names.Count; x++)
                        {
                            string value = Rows[y][x];
txtstream.WriteLine("Response.Write(\"<td>" + value + "</td>\" +
vbcrlf)");
                        }
txtstream.WriteLine("Response.Write(\"</tr>\" + vbcrlf)");
                    }
                    break;
                }
            case "Single-Line Vertical":
                {
                    for (int y = 0; y < Rows.Count; y++)
                    {
                        for (int x = 0; x < Names.Count; x++)
                        {
```

```
txtstream.WriteLine("Response.Write(\"<tr><th>" + Names[x] +
"</th><td>" + Rows[y][x] + "</td></tr>\" + vbcrlf)");
                        }
                        break;
                    }
                    break;
                }

            case "Multi-Line Vertical":
                {

                    for (int x = 0; x < Names.Count; x++)
                    {

txtstream.WriteLine("Response.Write(\"<tr><th>" + Names[x] +
"</th>\" + vbcrlf)");
                        for (int y = 0; y < Rows.Count; y++)
                        {
                            string value = Rows[y][x];

txtstream.WriteLine("Response.Write(\"<td>" + value + "</td>\" +
vbcrlf)");
                        }

txtstream.WriteLine("Response.Write(\"</tr>\" + vbcrlf)");
                    }
                    break;
                }


        }
        txtstream.WriteLine("Response.Write(\"</table>\" +
vbcrlf)");
            txtstream.WriteLine("%>");
            txtstream.WriteLine("</body>");
            txtstream.WriteLine("</html>");
            txtstream.Close();
        }
```

CREATE ASPX CODE

Inside this sub routine is the code to create an ASPX Webpage.

```
private void Create_ASPX_Code()
{
        Scripting.FileSystemObject fso = new
Scripting.FileSystemObject();
        Scripting.TextStream txtstream =
fso.OpenTextFile(System.Environment.CurrentDirectory +
"\\Process.aspx", Scripting.IOMode.ForWriting, true,
Scripting.Tristate.TristateUseDefault);
        txtstream.WriteLine("<!DOCTYPE html PUBLIC \"-
//W3C//DTD XHTML 1.0 Transitional//EN\"
\"http://www.w3.org/TR/xhtml1/DTD/xhtml1-transitional.dtd\">");
        txtstream.WriteLine("");
        txtstream.WriteLine("<html
xmlns=\"http://www.w3.org/1999/xhtml\">");
        txtstream.WriteLine("<head>");
        txtstream.WriteLine("<title>Win32_Process</title>");
        txtstream.WriteLine("<style type='text/css'>");
        txtstream.WriteLine("body");
        txtstream.WriteLine("{");
        txtstream.WriteLine("    PADDING-RIGHT: 0px;");
        txtstream.WriteLine("    PADDING-LEFT: 0px;");
        txtstream.WriteLine("    PADDING-BOTTOM: 0px;");
        txtstream.WriteLine("    MARGIN: 0px;");
        txtstream.WriteLine("    COLOR: #333;");
        txtstream.WriteLine("    PADDING-TOP: 0px;");
        txtstream.WriteLine("    FONT-FAMILY: verdana, arial,
helvetica, sans-serif;");
        txtstream.WriteLine("}");
        txtstream.WriteLine("table");
        txtstream.WriteLine("{");
        txtstream.WriteLine("    BORDER-RIGHT: #999999 1px
solid;");
        txtstream.WriteLine("    PADDING-RIGHT: 1px;");
```

```
        txtstream.WriteLine("    PADDING-LEFT: 1px;");
        txtstream.WriteLine("    PADDING-BOTTOM: 1px;");
        txtstream.WriteLine("    LINE-HEIGHT: 8px;");
        txtstream.WriteLine("    PADDING-TOP: 1px;");
        txtstream.WriteLine("    BORDER-BOTTOM: #999 1px
solid;");
        txtstream.WriteLine("    BACKGROUND-COLOR:
#eeeeee;");
        txtstream.WriteLine("
filter:progid:DXImageTransform.Microsoft.Shadow(color='silver',
Direction=135, Strength=16)");
        txtstream.WriteLine("}");
        txtstream.WriteLine("th");
        txtstream.WriteLine("{");
        txtstream.WriteLine("    BORDER-RIGHT: #999999 3px
solid;");
        txtstream.WriteLine("    PADDING-RIGHT: 6px;");
        txtstream.WriteLine("    PADDING-LEFT: 6px;");
        txtstream.WriteLine("    FONT-WEIGHT: Bold;");
        txtstream.WriteLine("    FONT-SIZE: 14px;");
        txtstream.WriteLine("    PADDING-BOTTOM: 6px;");
        txtstream.WriteLine("    COLOR: darkred;");
        txtstream.WriteLine("    LINE-HEIGHT: 14px;");
        txtstream.WriteLine("    PADDING-TOP: 6px;");
        txtstream.WriteLine("    BORDER-BOTTOM: #999 1px
solid;");
        txtstream.WriteLine("    BACKGROUND-COLOR:
#eeeeee;");
        txtstream.WriteLine("    FONT-FAMILY: font-family:
Cambria, serif;");
        txtstream.WriteLine("    FONT-SIZE: 12px;");
        txtstream.WriteLine("    text-align: left;");
        txtstream.WriteLine("    white-Space: nowrap;");
        txtstream.WriteLine("}");
        txtstream.WriteLine(".th");
        txtstream.WriteLine("{");
        txtstream.WriteLine("    BORDER-RIGHT: #999999 2px
solid;");
        txtstream.WriteLine("    PADDING-RIGHT: 6px;");
        txtstream.WriteLine("    PADDING-LEFT: 6px;");
        txtstream.WriteLine("    FONT-WEIGHT: Bold;");
        txtstream.WriteLine("    PADDING-BOTTOM: 6px;");
        txtstream.WriteLine("    COLOR: black;");
        txtstream.WriteLine("    PADDING-TOP: 6px;");
```

```
            txtstream.WriteLine("    BORDER-BOTTOM: #999 2px
solid;");
            txtstream.WriteLine("    BACKGROUND-COLOR:
#eeeeee;");
            txtstream.WriteLine("    FONT-FAMILY: font-family:
Cambria, serif;");
            txtstream.WriteLine("    FONT-SIZE: 10px;");
            txtstream.WriteLine("    text-align: right;");
            txtstream.WriteLine("    white-Space: nowrap;");
            txtstream.WriteLine("}");
            txtstream.WriteLine("td");
            txtstream.WriteLine("{");
            txtstream.WriteLine("    BORDER-RIGHT: #999999 3px
solid;");
            txtstream.WriteLine("    PADDING-RIGHT: 6px;");
            txtstream.WriteLine("    PADDING-LEFT: 6px;");
            txtstream.WriteLine("    FONT-WEIGHT: Normal;");
            txtstream.WriteLine("    PADDING-BOTTOM: 6px;");
            txtstream.WriteLine("    COLOR: navy;");
            txtstream.WriteLine("    LINE-HEIGHT: 14px;");
            txtstream.WriteLine("    PADDING-TOP: 6px;");
            txtstream.WriteLine("    BORDER-BOTTOM: #999 1px
solid;");
            txtstream.WriteLine("    BACKGROUND-COLOR:
#eeeeee;");
            txtstream.WriteLine("    FONT-FAMILY: font-family:
Cambria, serif;");
            txtstream.WriteLine("    FONT-SIZE: 12px;");
            txtstream.WriteLine("    text-align: left;");
            txtstream.WriteLine("    white-Space: nowrap;");
            txtstream.WriteLine("}");
            txtstream.WriteLine("div");
            txtstream.WriteLine("{");
            txtstream.WriteLine("    BORDER-RIGHT: #999999 3px
solid;");
            txtstream.WriteLine("    PADDING-RIGHT: 6px;");
            txtstream.WriteLine("    PADDING-LEFT: 6px;");
            txtstream.WriteLine("    FONT-WEIGHT: Normal;");
            txtstream.WriteLine("    PADDING-BOTTOM: 6px;");
            txtstream.WriteLine("    COLOR: white;");
            txtstream.WriteLine("    PADDING-TOP: 6px;");
            txtstream.WriteLine("    BORDER-BOTTOM: #999 1px
solid;");
            txtstream.WriteLine("    BACKGROUND-COLOR: navy;");
```

```
            txtstream.WriteLine("    FONT-FAMILY: font-family:
Cambria, serif;");
            txtstream.WriteLine("    FONT-SIZE: 10px;");
            txtstream.WriteLine("    text-align: left;");
            txtstream.WriteLine("    white-Space: nowrap;");
            txtstream.WriteLine("}");
            txtstream.WriteLine("span");
            txtstream.WriteLine("{");
            txtstream.WriteLine("    BORDER-RIGHT: #999999 3px
solid;");
            txtstream.WriteLine("    PADDING-RIGHT: 3px;");
            txtstream.WriteLine("    PADDING-LEFT: 3px;");
            txtstream.WriteLine("    FONT-WEIGHT: Normal;");
            txtstream.WriteLine("    PADDING-BOTTOM: 3px;");
            txtstream.WriteLine("    COLOR: white;");
            txtstream.WriteLine("    PADDING-TOP: 3px;");
            txtstream.WriteLine("    BORDER-BOTTOM: #999 1px
solid;");
            txtstream.WriteLine("    BACKGROUND-COLOR: navy;");
            txtstream.WriteLine("    FONT-FAMILY: font-family:
Cambria, serif;");
            txtstream.WriteLine("    FONT-SIZE: 10px;");
            txtstream.WriteLine("    text-align: left;");
            txtstream.WriteLine("    white-Space: nowrap;");
            txtstream.WriteLine("    display: inline-block;");
            txtstream.WriteLine("    width: 100%;");
            txtstream.WriteLine("}");
            txtstream.WriteLine("textarea");
            txtstream.WriteLine("{");
            txtstream.WriteLine("    BORDER-RIGHT: #999999 3px
solid;");
            txtstream.WriteLine("    PADDING-RIGHT: 3px;");
            txtstream.WriteLine("    PADDING-LEFT: 3px;");
            txtstream.WriteLine("    FONT-WEIGHT: Normal;");
            txtstream.WriteLine("    PADDING-BOTTOM: 3px;");
            txtstream.WriteLine("    COLOR: white;");
            txtstream.WriteLine("    PADDING-TOP: 3px;");
            txtstream.WriteLine("    BORDER-BOTTOM: #999 1px
solid;");
            txtstream.WriteLine("    BACKGROUND-COLOR: navy;");
            txtstream.WriteLine("    FONT-FAMILY: font-family:
Cambria, serif;");
            txtstream.WriteLine("    FONT-SIZE: 10px;");
            txtstream.WriteLine("    text-align: left;");
            txtstream.WriteLine("    white-Space: nowrap;");
```

```
txtstream.WriteLine("    width: 100%;");
txtstream.WriteLine("}");
txtstream.WriteLine("select");
txtstream.WriteLine("{");
txtstream.WriteLine("    BORDER-RIGHT: #999999 3px
solid;");
txtstream.WriteLine("    PADDING-RIGHT: 6px;");
txtstream.WriteLine("    PADDING-LEFT: 6px;");
txtstream.WriteLine("    FONT-WEIGHT: Normal;");
txtstream.WriteLine("    PADDING-BOTTOM: 6px;");
txtstream.WriteLine("    COLOR: white;");
txtstream.WriteLine("    PADDING-TOP: 6px;");
txtstream.WriteLine("    BORDER-BOTTOM: #999 1px
solid;");
txtstream.WriteLine("    BACKGROUND-COLOR: navy;");
txtstream.WriteLine("    FONT-FAMILY: font-family:
Cambria, serif;");
txtstream.WriteLine("    FONT-SIZE: 10px;");
txtstream.WriteLine("    text-align: left;");
txtstream.WriteLine("    white-Space: nowrap;");
txtstream.WriteLine("    width: 100%;");
txtstream.WriteLine("}");
txtstream.WriteLine("input");
txtstream.WriteLine("{");
txtstream.WriteLine("    BORDER-RIGHT: #999999 3px
solid;");
txtstream.WriteLine("    PADDING-RIGHT: 3px;");
txtstream.WriteLine("    PADDING-LEFT: 3px;");
txtstream.WriteLine("    FONT-WEIGHT: Bold;");
txtstream.WriteLine("    PADDING-BOTTOM: 3px;");
txtstream.WriteLine("    COLOR: white;");
txtstream.WriteLine("    PADDING-TOP: 3px;");
txtstream.WriteLine("    BORDER-BOTTOM: #999 1px
solid;");
txtstream.WriteLine("    BACKGROUND-COLOR: navy;");
txtstream.WriteLine("    FONT-FAMILY: font-family:
Cambria, serif;");
txtstream.WriteLine("    FONT-SIZE: 12px;");
txtstream.WriteLine("    text-align: left;");
txtstream.WriteLine("    display: table-cell;");
txtstream.WriteLine("    white-Space: nowrap;");
txtstream.WriteLine("    width: 100%;");
txtstream.WriteLine("}");
txtstream.WriteLine("h1 {");
txtstream.WriteLine("color: antiquewhite;");
```

```
            txtstream.WriteLine("text-shadow: 1px 1px 1px
black;");
            txtstream.WriteLine("padding: 3px;");
            txtstream.WriteLine("text-align: center;");
            txtstream.WriteLine("box-shadow: inset 2px 2px 5px
rgba(0,0,0,0.5), inset -2px -2px 5px rgba(255,255,255,0.5)");
            txtstream.WriteLine("}");
            txtstream.WriteLine("</style>");
            txtstream.WriteLine("</head>");
            txtstream.WriteLine("<body>");
            txtstream.WriteLine("<%");
            txtstream.WriteLine("Response.Write(\"<table
Border='1' cellpadding='1' cellspacing='1'>\" + vbcrlf)");


            switch (Orientation)
            {


                case "Single-Line Horizontal":
                    {
                        for (int y = 0; y < Rows.Count; y++)
                        {
txtstream.WriteLine("Response.Write(\"<tr>\" + vbcrlf)");
                            for (int x = 0; x < Names.Count; x++)
                            {
txtstream.WriteLine("Response.Write(\"<th>" + Names[x] + "</th>\"
+ vbcrlf)");
                            }

txtstream.WriteLine("Response.Write(\"</tr>\" + vbcrlf)");

txtstream.WriteLine("Response.Write(\"<tr>\" + vbcrlf)");
                            for (int x = 0; x < Names.Count; x++)
                            {
                                String value = Rows[y][x];

txtstream.WriteLine("Response.Write(\"<td>" + value + "</td>\" +
vbcrlf)");
                            }

txtstream.WriteLine("Response.Write(\"</tr>\" + vbcrlf)");
                        break;
```

```csharp
                    }
                    break;
                }

            case "Multi-Line Horizontal":
                {

                    for (int y = 0; y < Rows.Count; y++)
                    {

txtstream.WriteLine("Response.Write(\"<tr>\" + vbcrlf)");
                        for (int x = 0; x < Names.Count; x++)
                        {

txtstream.WriteLine("Response.Write(\"<th>" + Names[x] + "</th>\"
+ vbcrlf)");
                        }

txtstream.WriteLine("Response.Write(\"</tr>\" + vbcrlf)");
                        break;
                    }
                    for (int y = 0; y < Rows.Count; y++)
                    {

txtstream.WriteLine("Response.Write(\"<tr>\" + vbcrlf)");
                        for (int x = 0; x < Names.Count; x++)
                        {
                            string value = Rows[y][x];

txtstream.WriteLine("Response.Write(\"<td>" + value + "</td>\" +
vbcrlf)");
                        }

txtstream.WriteLine("Response.Write(\"</tr>\" + vbcrlf)");
                    }
                    break;
                }
            case "Single-Line Vertical":
                {

                    for (int y = 0; y < Rows.Count; y++)
                    {

                        for (int x = 0; x < Names.Count; x++)
                        {
```

```csharp
txtstream.WriteLine("Response.Write(\"<tr><th>" + Names[x] +
"</th><td>" + Rows[y][x] + "</td></tr>\" + vbcrlf)");
                                }
                            break;
                        }
                        break;
                }

            case "Multi-Line Vertical":
                {

                    for (int x = 0; x < Names.Count; x++)
                    {

txtstream.WriteLine("Response.Write(\"<tr><th>" + Names[x] +
"</th>\" + vbcrlf)");
                        for (int y = 0; y < Rows.Count; y++)
                        {
                            string value = Rows[y][x];

txtstream.WriteLine("Response.Write(\"<td>" + value + "</td>\" +
vbcrlf)");
                        }

txtstream.WriteLine("Response.Write(\"</tr>\" + vbcrlf)");
                    }
                    break;
                }

        }
        txtstream.WriteLine("Response.Write(\"</table>\" +
vbcrlf)");
        txtstream.WriteLine("%>");
        txtstream.WriteLine("</body>");
        txtstream.WriteLine("</html>");
        txtstream.Close();
        txtstream.WriteLine("</body>");
        txtstream.WriteLine("</html>");
        txtstream.Close();
    }
```

CREATE HTA CODE

Inside this sub routine is the code to create an HTA Application.

```
private void Create_HTA_Code()
{

        Scripting.FileSystemObject fso = new
Scripting.FileSystemObject();
        Scripting.TextStream txtstream =
fso.OpenTextFile(System.Environment.CurrentDirectory +
"\\Process.hta", Scripting.IOMode.ForWriting, true,
Scripting.Tristate.TristateUseDefault);
        txtstream.WriteLine("<html>");
        txtstream.WriteLine("<head>");
        txtstream.WriteLine("<HTA:APPLICATION ");
        txtstream.WriteLine("ID = \"Process\" ");
        txtstream.WriteLine("APPLICATIONNAME = \"Process\"
");
        txtstream.WriteLine("SCROLL = \"yes\" ");
        txtstream.WriteLine("SINGLEINSTANCE = \"yes\" ");
        txtstream.WriteLine("WINDOWSTATE = \"maximize\" >");
        txtstream.WriteLine("<title>Win32_Process</title>");
        txtstream.WriteLine("<style type='text/css'>");
        txtstream.WriteLine("body");
        txtstream.WriteLine("{");
        txtstream.WriteLine("    PADDING-RIGHT: 0px;");
        txtstream.WriteLine("    PADDING-LEFT: 0px;");
        txtstream.WriteLine("    PADDING-BOTTOM: 0px;");
        txtstream.WriteLine("    MARGIN: 0px;");
        txtstream.WriteLine("    COLOR: #333;");
        txtstream.WriteLine("    PADDING-TOP: 0px;");
        txtstream.WriteLine("    FONT-FAMILY: verdana, arial,
helvetica, sans-serif;");
        txtstream.WriteLine("}");
        txtstream.WriteLine("table");
        txtstream.WriteLine("{");
        txtstream.WriteLine("    BORDER-RIGHT: #999999 1px
solid;");
```

```
            txtstream.WriteLine("    PADDING-RIGHT: 1px;");
            txtstream.WriteLine("    PADDING-LEFT: 1px;");
            txtstream.WriteLine("    PADDING-BOTTOM: 1px;");
            txtstream.WriteLine("    LINE-HEIGHT: 8px;");
            txtstream.WriteLine("    PADDING-TOP: 1px;");
            txtstream.WriteLine("    BORDER-BOTTOM: #999 1px
solid;");
            txtstream.WriteLine("    BACKGROUND-COLOR:
#eeeeee;");
            txtstream.WriteLine("
filter:progid:DXImageTransform.Microsoft.Shadow(color='silver',
Direction=135, Strength=16)");
            txtstream.WriteLine("}");
            txtstream.WriteLine("th");
            txtstream.WriteLine("{");
            txtstream.WriteLine("    BORDER-RIGHT: #999999 3px
solid;");
            txtstream.WriteLine("    PADDING-RIGHT: 6px;");
            txtstream.WriteLine("    PADDING-LEFT: 6px;");
            txtstream.WriteLine("    FONT-WEIGHT: Bold;");
            txtstream.WriteLine("    FONT-SIZE: 14px;");
            txtstream.WriteLine("    PADDING-BOTTOM: 6px;");
            txtstream.WriteLine("    COLOR: darkred;");
            txtstream.WriteLine("    LINE-HEIGHT: 14px;");
            txtstream.WriteLine("    PADDING-TOP: 6px;");
            txtstream.WriteLine("    BORDER-BOTTOM: #999 1px
solid;");
            txtstream.WriteLine("    BACKGROUND-COLOR:
#eeeeee;");
            txtstream.WriteLine("    FONT-FAMILY: font-family:
Cambria, serif;");
            txtstream.WriteLine("    FONT-SIZE: 12px;");
            txtstream.WriteLine("    text-align: left;");
            txtstream.WriteLine("    white-Space: nowrap;");
            txtstream.WriteLine("}");
            txtstream.WriteLine(".th");
            txtstream.WriteLine("{");
            txtstream.WriteLine("    BORDER-RIGHT: #999999 2px
solid;");
            txtstream.WriteLine("    PADDING-RIGHT: 6px;");
            txtstream.WriteLine("    PADDING-LEFT: 6px;");
            txtstream.WriteLine("    FONT-WEIGHT: Bold;");
            txtstream.WriteLine("    PADDING-BOTTOM: 6px;");
            txtstream.WriteLine("    COLOR: black;");
            txtstream.WriteLine("    PADDING-TOP: 6px;");
```

```
            txtstream.WriteLine("    BORDER-BOTTOM: #999 2px
solid;");
            txtstream.WriteLine("    BACKGROUND-COLOR:
#eeeeee;");
            txtstream.WriteLine("    FONT-FAMILY: font-family:
Cambria, serif;");
            txtstream.WriteLine("    FONT-SIZE: 10px;");
            txtstream.WriteLine("    text-align: right;");
            txtstream.WriteLine("    white-Space: nowrap;");
            txtstream.WriteLine("}");
            txtstream.WriteLine("td");
            txtstream.WriteLine("{");
            txtstream.WriteLine("    BORDER-RIGHT: #999999 3px
solid;");
            txtstream.WriteLine("    PADDING-RIGHT: 6px;");
            txtstream.WriteLine("    PADDING-LEFT: 6px;");
            txtstream.WriteLine("    FONT-WEIGHT: Normal;");
            txtstream.WriteLine("    PADDING-BOTTOM: 6px;");
            txtstream.WriteLine("    COLOR: navy;");
            txtstream.WriteLine("    LINE-HEIGHT: 14px;");
            txtstream.WriteLine("    PADDING-TOP: 6px;");
            txtstream.WriteLine("    BORDER-BOTTOM: #999 1px
solid;");
            txtstream.WriteLine("    BACKGROUND-COLOR:
#eeeeee;");
            txtstream.WriteLine("    FONT-FAMILY: font-family:
Cambria, serif;");
            txtstream.WriteLine("    FONT-SIZE: 12px;");
            txtstream.WriteLine("    text-align: left;");
            txtstream.WriteLine("    white-Space: nowrap;");
            txtstream.WriteLine("}");
            txtstream.WriteLine("div");
            txtstream.WriteLine("{");
            txtstream.WriteLine("    BORDER-RIGHT: #999999 3px
solid;");
            txtstream.WriteLine("    PADDING-RIGHT: 6px;");
            txtstream.WriteLine("    PADDING-LEFT: 6px;");
            txtstream.WriteLine("    FONT-WEIGHT: Normal;");
            txtstream.WriteLine("    PADDING-BOTTOM: 6px;");
            txtstream.WriteLine("    COLOR: white;");
            txtstream.WriteLine("    PADDING-TOP: 6px;");
            txtstream.WriteLine("    BORDER-BOTTOM: #999 1px
solid;");
            txtstream.WriteLine("    BACKGROUND-COLOR: navy;");
```

```
            txtstream.WriteLine("    FONT-FAMILY: font-family:
Cambria, serif;");
            txtstream.WriteLine("    FONT-SIZE: 10px;");
            txtstream.WriteLine("    text-align: left;");
            txtstream.WriteLine("    white-Space: nowrap;");
            txtstream.WriteLine("}");
            txtstream.WriteLine("span");
            txtstream.WriteLine("{");
            txtstream.WriteLine("    BORDER-RIGHT: #999999 3px
solid;");
            txtstream.WriteLine("    PADDING-RIGHT: 3px;");
            txtstream.WriteLine("    PADDING-LEFT: 3px;");
            txtstream.WriteLine("    FONT-WEIGHT: Normal;");
            txtstream.WriteLine("    PADDING-BOTTOM: 3px;");
            txtstream.WriteLine("    COLOR: white;");
            txtstream.WriteLine("    PADDING-TOP: 3px;");
            txtstream.WriteLine("    BORDER-BOTTOM: #999 1px
solid;");
            txtstream.WriteLine("    BACKGROUND-COLOR: navy;");
            txtstream.WriteLine("    FONT-FAMILY: font-family:
Cambria, serif;");
            txtstream.WriteLine("    FONT-SIZE: 10px;");
            txtstream.WriteLine("    text-align: left;");
            txtstream.WriteLine("    white-Space: nowrap;");
            txtstream.WriteLine("    display: inline-block;");
            txtstream.WriteLine("    width: 100%;");
            txtstream.WriteLine("}");
            txtstream.WriteLine("textarea");
            txtstream.WriteLine("{");
            txtstream.WriteLine("    BORDER-RIGHT: #999999 3px
solid;");
            txtstream.WriteLine("    PADDING-RIGHT: 3px;");
            txtstream.WriteLine("    PADDING-LEFT: 3px;");
            txtstream.WriteLine("    FONT-WEIGHT: Normal;");
            txtstream.WriteLine("    PADDING-BOTTOM: 3px;");
            txtstream.WriteLine("    COLOR: white;");
            txtstream.WriteLine("    PADDING-TOP: 3px;");
            txtstream.WriteLine("    BORDER-BOTTOM: #999 1px
solid;");
            txtstream.WriteLine("    BACKGROUND-COLOR: navy;");
            txtstream.WriteLine("    FONT-FAMILY: font-family:
Cambria, serif;");
            txtstream.WriteLine("    FONT-SIZE: 10px;");
            txtstream.WriteLine("    text-align: left;");
            txtstream.WriteLine("    white-Space: nowrap;");
```

```
txtstream.WriteLine("    width: 100%;");
txtstream.WriteLine("}");
txtstream.WriteLine("select");
txtstream.WriteLine("{");
txtstream.WriteLine("    BORDER-RIGHT: #999999 3px
solid;");
txtstream.WriteLine("    PADDING-RIGHT: 6px;");
txtstream.WriteLine("    PADDING-LEFT: 6px;");
txtstream.WriteLine("    FONT-WEIGHT: Normal;");
txtstream.WriteLine("    PADDING-BOTTOM: 6px;");
txtstream.WriteLine("    COLOR: white;");
txtstream.WriteLine("    PADDING-TOP: 6px;");
txtstream.WriteLine("    BORDER-BOTTOM: #999 1px
solid;");
txtstream.WriteLine("    BACKGROUND-COLOR: navy;");
txtstream.WriteLine("    FONT-FAMILY: font-family:
Cambria, serif;");
txtstream.WriteLine("    FONT-SIZE: 10px;");
txtstream.WriteLine("    text-align: left;");
txtstream.WriteLine("    white-Space: nowrap;");
txtstream.WriteLine("    width: 100%;");
txtstream.WriteLine("}");
txtstream.WriteLine("input");
txtstream.WriteLine("{");
txtstream.WriteLine("    BORDER-RIGHT: #999999 3px
solid;");
txtstream.WriteLine("    PADDING-RIGHT: 3px;");
txtstream.WriteLine("    PADDING-LEFT: 3px;");
txtstream.WriteLine("    FONT-WEIGHT: Bold;");
txtstream.WriteLine("    PADDING-BOTTOM: 3px;");
txtstream.WriteLine("    COLOR: white;");
txtstream.WriteLine("    PADDING-TOP: 3px;");
txtstream.WriteLine("    BORDER-BOTTOM: #999 1px
solid;");
txtstream.WriteLine("    BACKGROUND-COLOR: navy;");
txtstream.WriteLine("    FONT-FAMILY: font-family:
Cambria, serif;");
txtstream.WriteLine("    FONT-SIZE: 12px;");
txtstream.WriteLine("    text-align: left;");
txtstream.WriteLine("    display: table-cell;");
txtstream.WriteLine("    white-Space: nowrap;");
txtstream.WriteLine("    width: 100%;");
txtstream.WriteLine("}");
txtstream.WriteLine("h1 {");
txtstream.WriteLine("color: antiquewhite;");
```

```
            txtstream.WriteLine("text-shadow: 1px 1px 1px
black;");
            txtstream.WriteLine("padding: 3px;");
            txtstream.WriteLine("text-align: center;");
            txtstream.WriteLine("box-shadow: inset 2px 2px 5px
rgba(0,0,0,0.5), inset -2px -2px 5px rgba(255,255,255,0.5)");
            txtstream.WriteLine("}");
            txtstream.WriteLine("</style>");
            txtstream.WriteLine("</head>");
            txtstream.WriteLine("<body>");
            txtstream.WriteLine("<table Border='1'
cellpadding='1' cellspacing='1'>");


            switch (Orientation)
            {


                case "Single-Line Horizontal":
                    {
                        for (int y = 0; y < Rows.Count; y++)
                        {
                            txtstream.WriteLine("<tr>");
                            for (int x = 0; x < Names.Count; x++)
                            {
                                txtstream.WriteLine("<th>" +
Names[x] + "</th>");
                            }
                            txtstream.WriteLine("</tr>");
                            txtstream.WriteLine("<tr>");
                            for (int x = 0; x < Names.Count; x++)
                            {
                                String value = Rows[y][x];
                                txtstream.WriteLine("<td>" +
value + "</td>");
                            }
                            txtstream.WriteLine("</tr>");
                            break;
                        }
                        break;
                    }
                case "Multi-Line Horizontal":
                    {
```

```
                    for (int y = 0; y < Rows.Count; y++)
                    {
                        txtstream.WriteLine("<tr>");
                        for (int x = 0; x < Names.Count; x++)
                        {
                            txtstream.WriteLine("<th>" +
Names[x] + "</th>");
                        }
                        txtstream.WriteLine("</tr>");
                        break;
                    ]
                    for (int y = 0; y < Rows.Count; y++)
                    {
                        txtstream.WriteLine("<tr>");
                        for (int x = 0; x < Names.Count; x++)
                        {
                            string value = Rows[y][x];
                            txtstream.WriteLine("<td>" +
value + "</td>");
                        }
                        txtstream.WriteLine("</tr>");
                    }
                    break;
                }
            case "Single-Line Vertical":
                {

                    for (int y = 0; y < Rows.Count; y++)
                    {

                        for (int x = 0; x < Names.Count; x++)
                        {
                            txtstream.WriteLine("<tr><th>" +
Names[x] + "</th><td>" + Rows[y][x] + "</td></tr>");
                        }
                        break;
                    }
                    break;
                }

            case "Multi-Line Vertical":
                {

                    for (int x = 0; x < Names.Count; x++)
                    {
```

```
                          txtstream.WriteLine("<tr><th>" +
Names[x] + "</th>");

                          for (int y = 0; y < Rows.Count; y++)
                          {
                              string value = Rows[y][x];
                              txtstream.WriteLine("<td>" +
value + "</td>");

                          }
                          txtstream.WriteLine("</tr>");
                    }
                    break;
              }

        }
        txtstream.WriteLine("</table>");
        txtstream.WriteLine("</body>");
        txtstream.WriteLine("</html>");
        txtstream.Close();
    }
```

CREATE HTML CODE

Inside this sub routine is the code to create an HTML Webpage that can be saved and displayed using the Web Browser control or saved and displayed at a later time.

```
private void Create_HTML_Code()
{

    Scripting.FileSystemObject fso = new
Scripting.FileSystemObject();
    Scripting.TextStream txtstream =
fso.OpenTextFile(System.Environment.CurrentDirectory +
"\\Process.html", Scripting.IOMode.ForWriting, true,
Scripting.Tristate.TristateUseDefault);
    txtstream.WriteLine("<html>");
    txtstream.WriteLine("<head>");
    txtstream.WriteLine("<title>Win32_Process</title>");
    txtstream.WriteLine("<style type='text/css'>");
    txtstream.WriteLine("body");
    txtstream.WriteLine("{");
    txtstream.WriteLine("    PADDING-RIGHT: 0px;");
    txtstream.WriteLine("    PADDING-LEFT: 0px;");
    txtstream.WriteLine("    PADDING-BOTTOM: 0px;");
    txtstream.WriteLine("    MARGIN: 0px;");
    txtstream.WriteLine("    COLOR: #333;");
    txtstream.WriteLine("    PADDING-TOP: 0px;");
    txtstream.WriteLine("    FONT-FAMILY: verdana, arial,
helvetica, sans-serif;");
    txtstream.WriteLine("}");
    txtstream.WriteLine("table");
    txtstream.WriteLine("{");
    txtstream.WriteLine("    BORDER-RIGHT: #999999 1px
solid;");
    txtstream.WriteLine("    PADDING-RIGHT: 1px;");
    txtstream.WriteLine("    PADDING-LEFT: 1px;");
    txtstream.WriteLine("    PADDING-BOTTOM: 1px;");
    txtstream.WriteLine("    LINE-HEIGHT: 8px;");
    txtstream.WriteLine("    PADDING-TOP: 1px;");
```

```
            txtstream.WriteLine("    BORDER-BOTTOM: #999 1px
solid;");
            txtstream.WriteLine("    BACKGROUND-COLOR:
#eeeeee;");
            txtstream.WriteLine("
filter:progid:DXImageTransform.Microsoft.Shadow(color='silver',
Direction=135, Strength=16)");
            txtstream.WriteLine("}");
            txtstream.WriteLine("th");
            txtstream.WriteLine("{");
            txtstream.WriteLine("    BORDER-RIGHT: #999999 3px
solid;");
            txtstream.WriteLine("    PADDING-RIGHT: 6px;");
            txtstream.WriteLine("    PADDING-LEFT: 6px;");
            txtstream.WriteLine("    FONT-WEIGHT: Bold;");
            txtstream.WriteLine("    FONT-SIZE: 14px;");
            txtstream.WriteLine("    PADDING-BOTTOM: 6px;");
            txtstream.WriteLine("    COLOR: darkred;");
            txtstream.WriteLine("    LINE-HEIGHT: 14px;");
            txtstream.WriteLine("    PADDING-TOP: 6px;");
            txtstream.WriteLine("    BORDER-BOTTOM: #999 1px
solid;");
            txtstream.WriteLine("    BACKGROUND-COLOR:
#eeeeee;");
            txtstream.WriteLine("    FONT-FAMILY: font-family:
Cambria, serif;");
            txtstream.WriteLine("    FONT-SIZE: 12px;");
            txtstream.WriteLine("    text-align: left;");
            txtstream.WriteLine("    white-Space: nowrap;");
            txtstream.WriteLine("}");
            txtstream.WriteLine(".th");
            txtstream.WriteLine("{");
            txtstream.WriteLine("    BORDER-RIGHT: #999999 2px
solid;");
            txtstream.WriteLine("    PADDING-RIGHT: 6px;");
            txtstream.WriteLine("    PADDING-LEFT: 6px;");
            txtstream.WriteLine("    FONT-WEIGHT: Bold;");
            txtstream.WriteLine("    PADDING-BOTTOM: 6px;");
            txtstream.WriteLine("    COLOR: black;");
            txtstream.WriteLine("    PADDING-TOP: 6px;");
            txtstream.WriteLine("    BORDER-BOTTOM: #999 2px
solid;");
            txtstream.WriteLine("    BACKGROUND-COLOR:
#eeeeee;");
```

```
            txtstream.WriteLine("    FONT-FAMILY: font-family:
Cambria, serif;");
            txtstream.WriteLine("    FONT-SIZE: 10px;");
            txtstream.WriteLine("    text-align: right;");
            txtstream.WriteLine("    white-Space: nowrap;");
            txtstream.WriteLine("}");
            txtstream.WriteLine("td");
            txtstream.WriteLine("{");
            txtstream.WriteLine("    BORDER-RIGHT: #999999 3px
solid;");
            txtstream.WriteLine("    PADDING-RIGHT: 6px;");
            txtstream.WriteLine("    PADDING-LEFT: 6px;");
            txtstream.WriteLine("    FONT-WEIGHT: Normal;");
            txtstream.WriteLine("    PADDING-BOTTOM: 6px;");
            txtstream.WriteLine("    COLOR: navy;");
            txtstream.WriteLine("    LINE-HEIGHT: 14px;");
            txtstream.WriteLine("    PADDING-TOP: 6px;");
            txtstream.WriteLine("    BORDER-BOTTOM: #999 1px
solid;");
            txtstream.WriteLine("    BACKGROUND-COLOR:
#eeeeee;");
            txtstream.WriteLine("    FONT-FAMILY: font-family:
Cambria, serif;");
            txtstream.WriteLine("    FONT-SIZE: 12px;");
            txtstream.WriteLine("    text-align: left;");
            txtstream.WriteLine("    white-Space: nowrap;");
            txtstream.WriteLine("}");
            txtstream.WriteLine("div");
            txtstream.WriteLine("{");
            txtstream.WriteLine("    BORDER-RIGHT: #999999 3px
solid;");
            txtstream.WriteLine("    PADDING-RIGHT: 6px;");
            txtstream.WriteLine("    PADDING-LEFT: 6px;");
            txtstream.WriteLine("    FONT-WEIGHT: Normal;");
            txtstream.WriteLine("    PADDING-BOTTOM: 6px;");
            txtstream.WriteLine("    COLOR: white;");
            txtstream.WriteLine("    PADDING-TOP: 6px;");
            txtstream.WriteLine("    BORDER-BOTTOM: #999 1px
solid;");
            txtstream.WriteLine("    BACKGROUND-COLOR: navy;");
            txtstream.WriteLine("    FONT-FAMILY: font-family:
Cambria, serif;");
            txtstream.WriteLine("    FONT-SIZE: 10px;");
            txtstream.WriteLine("    text-align: left;");
            txtstream.WriteLine("    white-Space: nowrap;");
```

```
            txtstream.WriteLine("}");
            txtstream.WriteLine("span");
            txtstream.WriteLine("{");
            txtstream.WriteLine("    BORDER-RIGHT: #999999 3px
solid;");
            txtstream.WriteLine("    PADDING-RIGHT: 3px;");
            txtstream.WriteLine("    PADDING-LEFT: 3px;");
            txtstream.WriteLine("    FONT-WEIGHT: Normal;");
            txtstream.WriteLine("    PADDING-BOTTOM: 3px;");
            txtstream.WriteLine("    COLOR: white;");
            txtstream.WriteLine("    PADDING-TOP: 3px;");
            txtstream.WriteLine("    BORDER-BOTTOM: #999 1px
solid;");
            txtstream.WriteLine("    BACKGROUND-COLOR: navy;");
            txtstream.WriteLine("    FONT-FAMILY: font-family:
Cambria, serif;");
            txtstream.WriteLine("    FONT-SIZE: 10px;");
            txtstream.WriteLine("    text-align: left;");
            txtstream.WriteLine("    white-Space: nowrap;");
            txtstream.WriteLine("    display: inline-block;");
            txtstream.WriteLine("    width: 100%;");
            txtstream.WriteLine("}");
            txtstream.WriteLine("textarea");
            txtstream.WriteLine("{");
            txtstream.WriteLine("    BORDER-RIGHT: #999999 3px
solid;");
            txtstream.WriteLine("    PADDING-RIGHT: 3px;");
            txtstream.WriteLine("    PADDING-LEFT: 3px;");
            txtstream.WriteLine("    FONT-WEIGHT: Normal;");
            txtstream.WriteLine("    PADDING-BOTTOM: 3px;");
            txtstream.WriteLine("    COLOR: white;");
            txtstream.WriteLine("    PADDING-TOP: 3px;");
            txtstream.WriteLine("    BORDER-BOTTOM: #999 1px
solid;");
            txtstream.WriteLine("    BACKGROUND-COLOR: navy;");
            txtstream.WriteLine("    FONT-FAMILY: font-family:
Cambria, serif;");
            txtstream.WriteLine("    FONT-SIZE: 10px;");
            txtstream.WriteLine("    text-align: left;");
            txtstream.WriteLine("    white-Space: nowrap;");
            txtstream.WriteLine("    width: 100%;");
            txtstream.WriteLine("}");
            txtstream.WriteLine("select");
            txtstream.WriteLine("{");
```

```
            txtstream.WriteLine("     BORDER-RIGHT: #999999 3px
solid;");
            txtstream.WriteLine("     PADDING-RIGHT: 6px;");
            txtstream.WriteLine("     PADDING-LEFT: 6px;");
            txtstream.WriteLine("     FONT-WEIGHT: Normal;");
            txtstream.WriteLine("     PADDING-BOTTOM: 6px;");
            txtstream.WriteLine("     COLOR: white;");
            txtstream.WriteLine("     PADDING-TOP: 6px;");
            txtstream.WriteLine("     BORDER-BOTTOM: #999 1px
solid;");
            txtstream.WriteLine("     BACKGROUND-COLOR: navy;");
            txtstream.WriteLine("     FONT-FAMILY: font-family:
Cambria, serif;");
            txtstream.WriteLine("     FONT-SIZE: 10px;");
            txtstream.WriteLine("     text-align: left;");
            txtstream.WriteLine("     white-Space: nowrap;");
            txtstream.WriteLine("     width: 100%;");
            txtstream.WriteLine("}");
            txtstream.WriteLine("input");
            txtstream.WriteLine("{");
            txtstream.WriteLine("     BORDER-RIGHT: #999999 3px
solid;");
            txtstream.WriteLine("     PADDING-RIGHT: 3px;");
            txtstream.WriteLine("     PADDING-LEFT: 3px;");
            txtstream.WriteLine("     FONT-WEIGHT: Bold;");
            txtstream.WriteLine("     PADDING-BOTTOM: 3px;");
            txtstream.WriteLine("     COLOR: white;");
            txtstream.WriteLine("     PADDING-TOP: 3px;");
            txtstream.WriteLine("     BORDER-BOTTOM: #999 1px
solid;");
            txtstream.WriteLine("     BACKGROUND-COLOR: navy;");
            txtstream.WriteLine("     FONT-FAMILY: font-family:
Cambria, serif;");
            txtstream.WriteLine("     FONT-SIZE: 12px;");
            txtstream.WriteLine("     text-align: left;");
            txtstream.WriteLine("     display: table-cell;");
            txtstream.WriteLine("     white-Space: nowrap;");
            txtstream.WriteLine("     width: 100%;");
            txtstream.WriteLine("}");
            txtstream.WriteLine("h1 {");
            txtstream.WriteLine("color: antiquewhite;");
            txtstream.WriteLine("text-shadow: 1px 1px 1px
black;");
            txtstream.WriteLine("padding: 3px;");
            txtstream.WriteLine("text-align: center;");
```

```csharp
            txtstream.WriteLine("box-shadow: inset 2px 2px 5px
rgba(0,0,0,0.5), inset -2px -2px 5px rgba(255,255,255,0.5)");
            txtstream.WriteLine("}");
            txtstream.WriteLine("</style>");
            txtstream.WriteLine("</head>");
            txtstream.WriteLine("<body>");
            txtstream.WriteLine("<table Border='1'
cellpadding='1' cellspacing='1'>");


            switch (Orientation)
            {

                case "Single-Line Horizontal":
                    {
                        for (int y = 0; y < Rows.Count; y++)
                        {
                            txtstream.WriteLine("<tr>");
                            for (int x = 0; x < Names.Count; x++)
                            {
                                txtstream.WriteLine("<th>" +
Names[x] + "</th>");

                            }
                            txtstream.WriteLine("</tr>");
                            txtstream.WriteLine("<tr>");
                            for (int x = 0; x < Names.Count; x++)
                            {
                                String value = Rows[y][x];
                                txtstream.WriteLine("<td>" +
value + "</td>");

                            }
                            txtstream.WriteLine("</tr>");
                            break;
                        }
                        break;
                    }

                case "Multi-Line Horizontal":
                    {

                        for (int y = 0; y < Rows.Count; y++)
                        {
                            txtstream.WriteLine("<tr>");
                            for (int x = 0; x < Names.Count; x++)
```

```
                            {
                                txtstream.WriteLine("<th>" +
Names[x] + "</th>");

                            }
                            txtstream.WriteLine("</tr>");
                            break;
                        }
                        for (int y = 0; y < Rows.Count; y++)
                        {
                            txtstream.WriteLine("<tr>");
                            for (int x = 0; x < Names.Count; x++)
                            {
                                string value = Rows[y][x];
                                txtstream.WriteLine("<td>" +
value + "</td>");

                            }
                            txtstream.WriteLine("</tr>");
                        }
                        break;
                    }
                case "Single-Line Vertical":
                    {

                        for (int y = 0; y < Rows.Count; y++)
                        {

                            for (int x = 0; x < Names.Count; x++)
                            {
                                txtstream.WriteLine("<tr><th>" +
Names[x] + "</th><td>" + Rows[y][x] + "</td></tr>");
                            }
                            break;
                        }
                        break;
                    }

                case "Multi-Line Vertical":
                    {

                        for (int x = 0; x < Names.Count; x++)
                        {

                            txtstream.WriteLine("<tr><th>" +
Names[x] + "</th>");
                            for (int y = 0; y < Rows.Count; y++)
```

```
                        {
                            string value = Rows[y][x];
                            txtstream.WriteLine("<td>" +
value + "</td>");

                        }
                        txtstream.WriteLine("</tr>");
                    }
                    break;
            }

        }
        txtstream.WriteLine("</table>");
        txtstream.WriteLine("</body>");
        txtstream.WriteLine("</html>");
        txtstream.Close();
    }
```

CREATE THE CSV FILE

Inside this sub routine is the code to create a CSV file. It is a separate routine because its extension –.csv – is seen by Excel – assuming it is installed as a text-based data file and knows what to do with it to display its contents.

```
        String tempstr = "";
        Scripting.FileSystemObject fso = new
Scripting.FileSystemObject();
        Scripting.TextStream txtstream =
fso.OpenTextFile(System.Environment.CurrentDirectory +
"\\Process.csv", Scripting.IOMode.ForWriting, true,
Scripting.Tristate.TristateUseDefault);

        switch (Orientation)
        {

            case "Single-Line Horizontal":
                {

                    for (int x = 0; x < Names.Count; x++)
                    {
                        if (tempstr != "")
                        {
                            tempstr = tempstr + ",";

                        }
                        tempstr = tempstr + Names[x];

                    }
                    txtstream.WriteLine(tempstr);
                    tempstr = "";

                    for (int y = 0; y < Rows.Count; y++)
                    {
                        for (int x = 0; x < Names.Count; x++)
                        {
```

```
                                    if (tempstr != "")
                                    {
                                        tempstr = tempstr + ",";
                                    }
                                    tempstr = tempstr + '"' +
Rows[y][x] + '"';

                                }
                            txtstream.WriteLine(tempstr);
                            tempstr = "";

                    }
                    txtstream.Close();

                    break;
                }
            case "Vertical":
                {

                    for (int x = 0; x < Names.Count; x++)
                    {
                        tempstr = Names[x];
                        for (int y = 0; y < Rows.Count; y++)
                        {

                            if (tempstr != "")
                            {
                                tempstr = tempstr + ",";
                            }
                            tempstr = tempstr + (char)34 +
Rows[y][x] + (char)34;

                        }
                        txtstream.WriteLine(tempstr);
                        tempstr = "";
                    }
                    break;

                }
            }

        }
```

CREATE THE EXCEL FILE

Inside this sub routine is the code to create a CSV file and then open it using an older version of Excel.

```
        String tempstr = "";
        Scripting.FileSystemObject fso = new
Scripting.FileSystemObject();
        Scripting.TextStream txtstream =
fso.OpenTextFile(System.Environment.CurrentDirectory +
"\\Process.csv", Scripting.IOMode.ForWriting, true,
Scripting.Tristate.TristateUseDefault);

        switch (Orientation)
        {

            case "Single-Line Horizontal":
                {

                    for (int x = 0; x < Names.Count; x++)
                    {
                        if (tempstr != "")
                        {
                            tempstr = tempstr + ",";

                        }
                        tempstr = tempstr + Names[x];

                    }
                    txtstream.WriteLine(tempstr);
                    tempstr = "";

                    for (int y = 0; y < Rows.Count; y++)
                    {
                        for (int x = 0; x < Names.Count; x++)
                        {
```

```
                                    if (tempstr != "")
                                    {
                                        tempstr = tempstr + ",";
                                    }
                                    tempstr = tempstr + '"' +
Rows[y][x] + '"';

                            }
                            txtstream.WriteLine(tempstr);
                            tempstr = "";

                    }
                    txtstream.Close();

                    break;
                }
            case "Vertical":
                {

                    for (int x = 0; x < Names.Count; x++)
                    {
                        tempstr = Names[x];
                        for (int y = 0; y < Rows.Count; y++)
                        {

                            if (tempstr != "")
                            {
                                tempstr = tempstr + ",";
                            }
                            tempstr = tempstr + (char)34 +
Rows[y][x] + (char)34;

                        }
                        txtstream.WriteLine(tempstr);
                        tempstr = "";
                    }
                    break;

                }
            }
        }
```

EXCEL AUTOMATION CODE

Inside this sub routine is the code to create an instance of Excel and populate a worksheet. Both horizontal and vertical orientations are available, and the code automatically aligns and autofits the cells.

```
public void Do_Excel_Automation_Code()
{
    Microsoft.Office.Interop.Excel.Application oExcel =
new Microsoft.Office.Interop.Excel.Application();
    Microsoft.Office.Interop.Excel.Workbook wb =
oExcel.Workbooks.Add();
    Microsoft.Office.Interop.Excel.Worksheet ws =
wb.Worksheets[0];
    switch (Orientation)
    {

        case "Horizontal":
            {
                for (int x = 0; x < Names.Count; x++)
                {
                    ws.Cells[1, x + 1] = Names[x];
                }
                for (int y = 0; y < Rows.Count; y++)
                {
                    for (int x = 0; x < Names.Count; x++)
                    {
                        ws.Cells[y + 2, x + 1] =
Rows[y][x];
                    }
                }
                break;
            }
        case "Vertical":
            {
```

```csharp
                    for (int x = 0; x < Names.Count; x++)
                    {
                        ws.Cells[x + 1, 1] = Names[x];
                    }
                    for (int y = 0; y < Rows.Count; y++)
                    {
                        for (int x = 0; x < Names.Count; x++)
                        {
                            ws.Cells[x + 1, y + 2] =
Rows[y][x];
                        }
                    }
                    break;
                }
        }
        ws.Columns.HorizontalAlignment =
Microsoft.Office.Interop.Excel.XlHAlign.xlHAlignLeft;
        ws.Columns.AutoFit();
    }
    public void Create_Text_File_Code()
    {

        String tempstr = "";
        Scripting.FileSystemObject fso = new
Scripting.FileSystemObject();
        Scripting.TextStream txtstream =
fso.OpenTextFile(System.Environment.CurrentDirectory +
"\\Process.xml", Scripting.IOMode.ForWriting, true,
Scripting.Tristate.TristateUseDefault);

        switch (Orientation)
        {

            case "Single-Line Horizontal":
                {

                    for (int x = 0; x < Names.Count; x++)
                    {
                        if (tempstr != "")
                        {
                            tempstr = tempstr + Delim;

                        }
                        tempstr = tempstr + Names[x];
```

```
                    }
                    txtstream.WriteLine(tempstr);
                    tempstr = "";

                    for (int y = 0; y < Rows.Count; y++)
                    {
                        for (int x = 0; x < Names.Count; x++)
                        {
                            if (tempstr != "")
                            {
                                tempstr = tempstr + Delim;
                            }
                            tempstr = tempstr + '"' +
Rows[y][x] + '"';

                        }
                        txtstream.WriteLine(tempstr);
                        tempstr = "";

                    }
                    txtstream.Close();

                    break;
                }
            case "Vertical":
                {

                    for (int x = 0; x < Names.Count; x++)
                    {
                        tempstr = Names[x];
                        for (int y = 0; y < Rows.Count; y++)
                        {

                            if (tempstr != "")
                            {
                                tempstr = tempstr + Delim;
                            }
                            tempstr = tempstr + (char)34 +
Rows[y][x] + (char)34;

                        }
                        txtstream.WriteLine(tempstr);
                        tempstr = "";
                    }
                    break;
```

```
                    }
            }

        }
```

CREATE CUSTOM
DELIMITED TEXT FILE

This sub routine is designed to provide you with maximum flexibility. You choose the orientation and the delimiter.

```
public void Create_Text_File_Code()
        {
            String tempstr = "";
            Scripting.FileSystemObject fso = new
Scripting.FileSystemObject();
            Scripting.TextStream txtstream =
fso.OpenTextFile(System.Environment.CurrentDirectory +
"\\Process.xml", Scripting.IOMode.ForWriting, true,
Scripting.Tristate.TristateUseDefault);

            switch (Orientation)
            {
                case "Single-Line Horizontal":
                    {
                        for (int x = 0; x < Names.Count; x++)
                        {
                            if (tempstr != "")
                            {
                                tempstr = tempstr + Delim;
```

```
                    }
                    tempstr = tempstr + Names[x];

                }
                txtstream.WriteLine(tempstr);
                tempstr = "";

                for (int y = 0; y < Rows.Count; y++)
                {
                    for (int x = 0; x < Names.Count; x++)
                    {
                        if (tempstr != "")
                        {
                            tempstr = tempstr + Delim;
                        }
                        tempstr = tempstr + '"' +
Rows[y][x] + '"';

                    }
                    txtstream.WriteLine(tempstr);
                    tempstr = "";

                }
                txtstream.Close();

                break;
            }
        case "Vertical":
            {

                for (int x = 0; x < Names.Count; x++)
                {
                    tempstr = Names[x];
                    for (int y = 0; y < Rows.Count; y++)
                    {

                        if (tempstr != "")
                        {
                            tempstr = tempstr + Delim;
                        }
                        tempstr = tempstr + (char)34 +
Rows[y][x] + (char)34;

                    }
                    txtstream.WriteLine(tempstr);
```

```
                tempstr = "";
            }
            break;

        }
    }

}
```

CREATE AN EXCEL SPREADSHEET TEXT FILE

Simply put, this routine creates an Excel Spreadsheet File that will automatically be displayed by Excel as a worksheet.

```
public void Create_Excel_SpreadSheet()
{
        Scripting.FileSystemObject fso = new
Scripting.FileSystemObject();
        Scripting.TextStream txtstream =
fso.OpenTextFile(System.Environment.CurrentDirectory +
"\\Process.xml", Scripting.IOMode.ForWriting, true,
Scripting.Tristate.TristateUseDefault);
        txtstream.WriteLine("<?xml version='1.0'?>");
        txtstream.WriteLine("<?mso-application
progid='Excel.Sheet'?>");
        txtstream.WriteLine("<Workbook xmlns='urn:schemas-
microsoft-com:office:spreadsheet' xmlns:o='urn:schemas-microsoft-
com:office:office' xmlns:x='urn:schemas-microsoft-
com:office:excel' xmlns:ss='urn:schemas-microsoft-
com:office:spreadsheet' xmlns:html='http://www.w3.org/TR/REC-
html40'>");
        txtstream.WriteLine("   <Documentproperties
xmlns='urn:schemas-microsoft-com:office:office'>");
        txtstream.WriteLine("        <Author>Windows
User</Author>");
        txtstream.WriteLine("        <LastAuthor>Windows
User</LastAuthor>");
        txtstream.WriteLine("        <Created>2007-11-
27T19:36:16Z</Created>");
        txtstream.WriteLine("        <Version>12.00</Version>");
        txtstream.WriteLine("   </Documentproperties>");
```

```
            txtstream.WriteLine("    <ExcelWorkbook
xmlns='urn:schemas-microsoft-com:office:excel'>");
            txtstream.WriteLine("
<WindowHeight>11835</WindowHeight>");
            txtstream.WriteLine("
<WindowWidth>18960</WindowWidth>");
            txtstream.WriteLine("
<WindowTopX>120</WindowTopX>");
            txtstream.WriteLine("
<WindowTopY>135</WindowTopY>");
            txtstream.WriteLine("
<ProtectStructure>False</ProtectStructure>");
            txtstream.WriteLine("
<ProtectWindows>False</ProtectWindows>");
            txtstream.WriteLine("    </ExcelWorkbook>");
            txtstream.WriteLine("    <Styles>");
            txtstream.WriteLine("        <Style ss:ID='Default'
ss:Name='Normal'>");
            txtstream.WriteLine("          <Alignment
ss:Vertical='Bottom'/>");
            txtstream.WriteLine("          <Borders/>");
            txtstream.WriteLine("          <Font
ss:FontName='Calibri' x:Family='Swiss' ss:Size='11'
ss:Color='#000000'/>");
            txtstream.WriteLine("          <Interior/>");
            txtstream.WriteLine("          <NumberFormat/>");
            txtstream.WriteLine("          <Protection/>");
            txtstream.WriteLine("        </Style>");
            txtstream.WriteLine("        <Style ss:ID='s62'>");
            txtstream.WriteLine("          <Borders/>");
            txtstream.WriteLine("          <Font
ss:FontName='Calibri' x:Family='Swiss' ss:Size='11'
ss:Color='#000000' ss:Bold='1'/>");
            txtstream.WriteLine("        </Style>");
            txtstream.WriteLine("        <Style ss:ID='s63'>");
            txtstream.WriteLine("          <Alignment
ss:Horizontal='Left' ss:Vertical='Bottom' ss:Indent='2'/>");
            txtstream.WriteLine("          <Font
ss:FontName='Verdana' x:Family='Swiss' ss:Size='7.7'
ss:Color='#000000'/>");
            txtstream.WriteLine("        </Style>");
            txtstream.WriteLine("    </Styles>");
            txtstream.WriteLine("<Worksheet ss:Name='Process'>");
            txtstream.WriteLine("    <Table x:FullColumns='1'
x:FullRows='1' ss:DefaultRowHeight='24.9375'>");
```

```
            txtstream.WriteLine("        <Column
ss:AutoFitWidth='1' ss:Width='82.5' ss:Span='5'/>");
            txtstream.WriteLine("        <Row
ss:AutoFitHeight='0'>");
            for (int x = 0; x < Names.Count; x++)
            {
                txtstream.WriteLine("        <Cell
ss:StyleID='s62'><Data ss:Type='String'>" + Names[x] +
"</Data></Cell>");
            }
            txtstream.WriteLine("        </Row>");
            for (int y = 0; y < Rows.Count; y++)
            {
                txtstream.WriteLine("        <Row
ss:AutoFitHeight='0' ss:Height='13.5'>");
                for (int x = 0; x < Names.Count; x++)
                {
                    txtstream.WriteLine("        <Cell><Data
ss:Type='String'><![CDATA[" + Rows[y][x] + "]]></Data></Cell>");
                }
                txtstream.WriteLine("        </Row>");
            }
            txtstream.WriteLine("    </Table>");
            txtstream.WriteLine("    <WorksheetOptions
xmlns='urn:schemas-microsoft-com:office:excel'>");
            txtstream.WriteLine("        <PageSetup>");
            txtstream.WriteLine("            <Header
x:Margin='0.3'/>");
            txtstream.WriteLine("            <Footer
x:Margin='0.3'/>");
            txtstream.WriteLine("            <PageMargins
x:Bottom='0.75' x:Left='0.7' x:Right='0.7' x:Top='0.75'/>");
            txtstream.WriteLine("        </PageSetup>");
            txtstream.WriteLine("        <Unsynced/>");
            txtstream.WriteLine("        <Print>");
            txtstream.WriteLine("
<FitHeight>0</FitHeight>");
            txtstream.WriteLine("
<ValidPrinterInfo/>");
            txtstream.WriteLine("
<HorizontalResolution>600</HorizontalResolution>");
            txtstream.WriteLine("
<VerticalResolution>600</VerticalResolution>");
            txtstream.WriteLine("        </Print>");
            txtstream.WriteLine("        <Selected/>");
```

```
            txtstream.WriteLine("          <Panes>");
            txtstream.WriteLine("            <Pane>");
            txtstream.WriteLine("
<Number>3</Number>");
            txtstream.WriteLine("
<ActiveRow>9</ActiveRow>");
            txtstream.WriteLine("
<ActiveCol>7</ActiveCol>");
            txtstream.WriteLine("            </Pane>");
            txtstream.WriteLine("          </Panes>");
            txtstream.WriteLine("
<ProtectObjects>False</ProtectObjects>");
            txtstream.WriteLine("
<ProtectScenarios>False</ProtectScenarios>");
            txtstream.WriteLine("   </WorksheetOptions>");
            txtstream.WriteLine("</Worksheet>");
            txtstream.WriteLine("</Workbook>");
            txtstream.Close();

        }
```

CREATE AN XML FILE

This sub routine creates a very simple Element XML File. This file can be used with the MSDAOSP and therefore, becomes as database text file.

```
public void Create_Element_XML_Code()
{


        Scripting.FileSystemObject fso = new
Scripting.FileSystemObject();
        Scripting.TextStream txtstream =
fso.OpenTextFile(System.Environment.CurrentDirectory +
"\\Process.xml", Scripting.IOMode.ForWriting, true,
Scripting.Tristate.TristateUseDefault);
        txtstream.WriteLine("<?xml version='1.0'
encoding='iso-8859-1'?>");
        txtstream.WriteLine("<data>");
        for (int y = 0; y < Rows.Count; y++)
        {
            txtstream.WriteLine("<Win32_process>");
            for (int x = 0; x < Names.Count; x++)
            {
                txtstream.WriteLine("<" + Names[x] + ">" +
Rows[y][x] + "</" + Names[x] + ">");
            }
            txtstream.WriteLine("</Win32_process>");
        }
        txtstream.WriteLine("</data>");
        txtstream.Close();

}
```

CREATE AN XML FOR XSL FILE

```
public void Create_Element_XML_For_XSL_Files_Code()
{

        Scripting.FileSystemObject fso = new
Scripting.FileSystemObject();
        Scripting.TextStream txtstream =
fso.OpenTextFile(System.Environment.CurrentDirectory +
"\\Process.xml", Scripting.IOMode.ForWriting, true,
Scripting.Tristate.TristateUseDefault);
        txtstream.WriteLine("<?xml version='1.0'
encoding='iso-8859-1'?>");
        txtstream.WriteLine("<?xml-stylesheet type='Text/xsl'
href='" + System.Environment.CurrentDirectory +
"\\Win32_Process.xsl'?>");
        txtstream.WriteLine("<data>");
        for (int y = 0; y < Rows.Count; y++)
        {
            txtstream.WriteLine("<Win32_process>");
            for (int x = 0; x < Names.Count; x++)
            {
                txtstream.WriteLine("<" + Names[x] + ">" +
Rows[y][x] + "</" + Names[x] + ">");
            }
            txtstream.WriteLine("</Win32_process>");
        }
        txtstream.WriteLine("</data>");
        txtstream.Close();

}
```

CREATE A SCHEMA XML

This sub routine creates a very simple Element XML File but is dependent upon the specified XSL file. It is opened by ADO and uses the MSDAOSP provider.

This file is then saved and can be used by the MSPERSIST provider.

```csharp
public void Create_Schema_XML_Files_Code()
{

        Scripting.FileSystemObject fso = new
Scripting.FileSystemObject();
        Scripting.TextStream txtstream =
fso.OpenTextFile(System.Environment.CurrentDirectory +
"\\Process.xml", Scripting.IOMode.ForWriting, true,
Scripting.Tristate.TristateUseDefault);
        txtstream.WriteLine("<?xml version='1.0'
encoding='iso-8859-1'?>");
        txtstream.WriteLine("<data>");
        for (int y = 0; y < Rows.Count; y++)
        {
            txtstream.WriteLine("<Win32_process>");
            for (int x = 0; x < Names.Count; x++)
            {
                txtstream.WriteLine("<" + Names[x] + ">" +
Rows[y][x] + "</" + Names[x] + ">");
            }
            txtstream.WriteLine("</Win32_process>");
        }
        txtstream.WriteLine("</data>");
        txtstream.Close();


        ADODB.Recordset rs1 = new ADODB.Recordset();
        rs1.ActiveConnection = "Provider=MSDAOSP; Data
Source=msxml2.DSOControl";
        rs1.Open(System.Environment.CurrentDirectory +
"\\Win32_Process.xml");
```

```
            if
(fso.FileExists(System.Environment.CurrentDirectory +
"\\Win32_Process_Schema.xml") == true)
            {

fso.DeleteFile(System.Environment.CurrentDirectory +
"\\Win32_Process_Schema.xml");
            }
            rs1.Save(System.Environment.CurrentDirectory +
"\\Win32_Process_Schema.xml", PersistFormatEnum.adPersistXML);

        }
```

CREATE THE XSL FILES

Inside this sub routine is the code to create the XSL File designed to render the XML as an HTML Webpage. It can be saved and displayed using the Web Browser control or saved and displayed at a later time. Simply pass in the collection generated by the Return_Management_Collection and specify its orientation.

```
public void Create_XSL_Files_Code()
{

    Scripting.FileSystemObject fso = new
Scripting.FileSystemObject();
    Scripting.TextStream txtstream =
fso.OpenTextFile(System.Environment.CurrentDirectory +
"\\Process.xsl", Scripting.IOMode.ForWriting, true,
Scripting.Tristate.TristateUseDefault);

    switch (Orientation)
    {

        case "Single-Line Horizontal":
            {
                txtstream.WriteLine("<?xml version='1.0'
encoding='UTF-8'?>");
                txtstream.WriteLine("<xsl:stylesheet
version='1.0'
xmlns:xsl='http://www.w3.org/1999/XSL/Transform'>");
                txtstream.WriteLine("<xsl:template
match=\"/\">");
                txtstream.WriteLine("<html>");
                txtstream.WriteLine("<head>");

txtstream.WriteLine("<title>Products</title>");
```

```
                        txtstream.WriteLine("<style
type='text/css'>");
                        txtstream.WriteLine("th");
                        txtstream.WriteLine("{");
                        txtstream.WriteLine("     COLOR:
darkred;");
                        txtstream.WriteLine("     BACKGROUND-
COLOR: white;");
                        txtstream.WriteLine("     FONT-
FAMILY:font-family: Cambria, serif;");
                        txtstream.WriteLine("     FONT-SIZE:
12px;");
                        txtstream.WriteLine("     text-align:
left;");
                        txtstream.WriteLine("     white-Space:
nowrap;");
                        txtstream.WriteLine("}");
                        txtstream.WriteLine("td");
                        txtstream.WriteLine("{");
                        txtstream.WriteLine("     COLOR: navy;");
                        txtstream.WriteLine("     BACKGROUND-
COLOR: white;");
                        txtstream.WriteLine("     FONT-FAMILY:
font-family: Cambria, serif;");
                        txtstream.WriteLine("     FONT-SIZE:
12px;");
                        txtstream.WriteLine("     text-align:
left;");
                        txtstream.WriteLine("     white-Space:
nowrap;");
                        txtstream.WriteLine("}");
                        txtstream.WriteLine("</style>");
                        txtstream.WriteLine("</head>");
                        txtstream.WriteLine("<body
bgcolor='#333333'>");
                        txtstream.WriteLine("<table
colspacing='3' colpadding='3'>");
                        txtstream.WriteLine("<tr>");
                        for (int x = 0; x < Names.Count; x++)
                        {
                            txtstream.WriteLine("<th>" + Names[x]
+ "</th>");
                        }
                        txtstream.WriteLine("</tr>");
                        txtstream.WriteLine("<tr>");
```

```
                    for (int x = 0; x < Names.Count; x++)
                    {
                        txtstream.WriteLine("<td><xsl:value-
of select=\"data/Win32_Process/" + Names[x] + "\"/></td>");
                    }
                    txtstream.WriteLine("</tr>");
                    txtstream.WriteLine("</table>");
                    txtstream.WriteLine("</body>");
                    txtstream.WriteLine("</html>");
                    txtstream.WriteLine("</xsl:template>");
                    txtstream.WriteLine("</xsl:stylesheet>");
                    txtstream.Close();

                    break;
                }
            case "Multi Line Horizontal":
                {

                    txtstream.WriteLine("<?xml version='1.0'
encoding='UTF-8'?>");
                    txtstream.WriteLine("<xsl:stylesheet
version='1.0'
xmlns:xsl='http://www.w3.org/1999/XSL/Transform'>");
                    txtstream.WriteLine("<xsl:template
match=\"/\">");

                    txtstream.WriteLine("<html>");
                    txtstream.WriteLine("<head>");

txtstream.WriteLine("<title>Products</title>");
                    txtstream.WriteLine("<style
type='text/css'>");
                    txtstream.WriteLine("th");
                    txtstream.WriteLine("{");
                    txtstream.WriteLine("   COLOR:
darkred;");
                    txtstream.WriteLine("   BACKGROUND-
COLOR: white;");
                    txtstream.WriteLine("   FONT-
FAMILY:font-family: Cambria, serif;");
                    txtstream.WriteLine("   FONT-SIZE:
12px;");
                    txtstream.WriteLine("   text-align:
left;");
                    txtstream.WriteLine("   white-Space:
nowrap;");
```

```csharp
                    txtstream.WriteLine("}");
                    txtstream.WriteLine("td");
                    txtstream.WriteLine("{");
                    txtstream.WriteLine("    COLOR: navy;");
                    txtstream.WriteLine("    BACKGROUND-
COLOR: white;");
                    txtstream.WriteLine("    FONT-FAMILY:
font-family: Cambria, serif;");
                    txtstream.WriteLine("    FONT-SIZE:
12px;");
                    txtstream.WriteLine("    text-align:
left;");
                    txtstream.WriteLine("    white-Space:
nowrap;");
                    txtstream.WriteLine("}");
                    txtstream.WriteLine("</style>");
                    txtstream.WriteLine("</head>");
                    txtstream.WriteLine("<body
bgcolor='#333333'>");
                    txtstream.WriteLine("<table
colspacing='3' colpadding='3'>");
                    txtstream.WriteLine("<tr>");
                    for (int x = 0; x < Names.Count; x++)
                    {
                        txtstream.WriteLine("<th>" + Names[x]
+ "</th>");
                    }
                    txtstream.WriteLine("</tr>");
                    txtstream.WriteLine("<xsl:for-each
select=\"data/Win32_Process\">");
                    txtstream.WriteLine("<tr>");
                    for (int x = 0; x < Names.Count; x++)
                    {
                        txtstream.WriteLine("<td><xsl:value-
of select=\"data/Win32_Process/" + Names[x] + "\"/></td>");
                    }
                    txtstream.WriteLine("</tr>");
                    txtstream.WriteLine("</xsl:for-each>");
                    txtstream.WriteLine("</table>");
                    txtstream.WriteLine("</body>");
                    txtstream.WriteLine("</html>");
                    txtstream.WriteLine("</xsl:template>");
                    txtstream.WriteLine("</xsl:stylesheet>");
                    txtstream.Close();
```

```
                        break;
                }
            case "Single Line Vertical":
                {
                        txtstream.WriteLine("<?xml version='1.0'
encoding='UTF-8'?>");
                        txtstream.WriteLine("<xsl:stylesheet
version='1.0'
xmlns:xsl='http://www.w3.org/1999/XSL/Transform'>");
                        txtstream.WriteLine("<xsl:template
match=\"/\">"),
                        txtstream.WriteLine("<html>");
                        txtstream.WriteLine("<head>");

txtstream.WriteLine("<title>Products</title>");
                        txtstream.WriteLine("<style
type='text/css'>");
                        txtstream.WriteLine("th");
                        txtstream.WriteLine("{");
                        txtstream.WriteLine("    COLOR:
darkred;");
                        txtstream.WriteLine("    BACKGROUND-
COLOR: white;");
                        txtstream.WriteLine("    FONT-
FAMILY:font-family: Cambria, serif;");
                        txtstream.WriteLine("    FONT-SIZE:
12px;");
                        txtstream.WriteLine("    text-align:
left;");
                        txtstream.WriteLine("    white-Space:
nowrap;");
                        txtstream.WriteLine("}");
                        txtstream.WriteLine("td");
                        txtstream.WriteLine("{");
                        txtstream.WriteLine("    COLOR: navy;");
                        txtstream.WriteLine("    BACKGROUND-
COLOR: white;");
                        txtstream.WriteLine("    FONT-FAMILY:
font-family: Cambria, serif;");
                        txtstream.WriteLine("    FONT-SIZE:
12px;");
                        txtstream.WriteLine("    text-align:
left;");
                        txtstream.WriteLine("    white-Space:
nowrap;");
```

```csharp
                      txtstream.WriteLine("}");
                      txtstream.WriteLine("</style>");
                      txtstream.WriteLine("</head>");
                      txtstream.WriteLine("<body
bgcolor='#333333'>");
                      txtstream.WriteLine("<table
colspacing='3' colpadding='3'>");
                      for (int x = 0; x < Names.Count; x++)
                      {
                            txtstream.WriteLine("<tr><th>" +
Names[x] + "</th>");
                            txtstream.WriteLine("<td><xsl:value-
of select=\"data/Win32_Process/" + Names[x] + "\"/></td></tr>");
                      }
                      txtstream.WriteLine("</table>");
                      txtstream.WriteLine("</body>");
                      txtstream.WriteLine("</html>");
                      txtstream.WriteLine("</xsl:template>");
                      txtstream.WriteLine("</xsl:stylesheet>");
                      txtstream.Close();

                      break;

                }
            case "Multi Line Vertical":
                {

                      txtstream.WriteLine("<?xml version='1.0'
encoding='UTF-8'?>");
                      txtstream.WriteLine("<xsl:stylesheet
version='1.0'
xmlns:xsl='http://www.w3.org/1999/XSL/Transform'>");
                      txtstream.WriteLine("<xsl:template
match=\"/\">");
                      txtstream.WriteLine("<html>");
                      txtstream.WriteLine("<head>");

txtstream.WriteLine("<title>Products</title>");
                      txtstream.WriteLine("<style
type='text/css'>");
                      txtstream.WriteLine("th");
                      txtstream.WriteLine("{");
                      txtstream.WriteLine("    COLOR:
darkred;");
```

```
                        txtstream.WriteLine("     BACKGROUND-
COLOR: white;");
                        txtstream.WriteLine("     FONT-
FAMILY:font-family: Cambria, serif;");
                        txtstream.WriteLine("     FONT-SIZE:
12px;");
                        txtstream.WriteLine("     text-align:
left;");
                        txtstream.WriteLine("     white-Space:
nowrap;");
                        txtstream.WriteLine("}"),
                        txtstream.WriteLine("td");
                        txtstream.WriteLine("{");
                        txtstream.WriteLine("     COLOR: navy;");
                        txtstream.WriteLine("     BACKGROUND-
COLOR: white;");
                        txtstream.WriteLine("     FONT-FAMILY:
font-family: Cambria, serif;");
                        txtstream.WriteLine("     FONT-SIZE:
12px;");
                        txtstream.WriteLine("     text-align:
left;");
                        txtstream.WriteLine("     white-Space:
nowrap;");
                        txtstream.WriteLine("}");
                        txtstream.WriteLine("</style>");
                        txtstream.WriteLine("</head>");
                        txtstream.WriteLine("<body
bgcolor='#333333'>");
                        txtstream.WriteLine("<table
colspacing='3' colpadding='3'>");
                        for (int x = 0; x < Names.Count; x++)
                        {
                            txtstream.WriteLine("<tr><th>" +
Names[x] + "</th>");
                            txtstream.WriteLine("<td><xsl:for-
each select=\"data/Win32_Process\">");
                            txtstream.WriteLine("<xsl:value-of
select=\"" + Names[x] + "\"/></td>");
                            txtstream.WriteLine("</xsl:for-
each></tr>");
                        }
                        txtstream.WriteLine("</table>");
                        txtstream.WriteLine("</body>");
                        txtstream.WriteLine("</html>");
```

```
            txtstream.WriteLine("</xsl:template>");
            txtstream.WriteLine("</xsl:stylesheet>");
            txtstream.Close();

            break;
        }
    }

}
```

THE GETVALUE FUNCTION

This is where a function called GetValue is the very first routine of the module and is used to return the value of the property in the row of an object collection. One of the first things I learned early on is that it is much easier to parse a string than to have to deal with converting a laundry list of property datatypes and react to the common datetime datatype. Either there is a value assigned to the Property or there isn't. Either that value is a datetime datatype or it isn't.

```csharp
private string GetValue(string N, ManagementObject obj)
{
    int pos = 0;
    string tN = N;
    string tempstr = obj.GetText(0);
    tN = tN + " = ";
    pos = tempstr.IndexOf(tN);
    if (pos > 0)
    {
        pos = pos + tN.Length;
        tempstr = tempstr.Substring(pos, tempstr.Length - pos);

        pos = tempstr.IndexOf(";");
        tempstr = tempstr.Substring(0, pos);
        tempstr = tempstr.Replace("{", "");
        tempstr = tempstr.Replace("}", "");
        tempstr = tempstr.Replace("\"", "");
        tempstr = tempstr.Trim();
        if (obj.Properties[N].Type == CimType.DateTime && tempstr.Length > 14)
        {
            return ReturnDateTime(tempstr);
        }
```

```
            else
            {
                return tempstr;
            }
        }
        else
        {
            return "";
        }
    }
    private string ReturnDateTime(string Value)
    {
        return Value.Substring(4, 2) + "/" +
Value.Substring(6, 2) + "/" + Value.Substring(0, 4) + " " +
Value.Substring(8, 2) + ":" + Value.Substring(10, 2) + ":" +
Value.Substring(12, 2);
    }

}
}
```

Stylesheets

The difference between boring and oh, wow!

The stylesheets in Appendix A, were used to render these pages. If you find one you like, feel free to use it.

Report:

OrderID	CustomerID	EmployeeID	OrderDate	RequiredDate	ShippedDate	ShipVia	Freight	ShipName	ShipAddress	ShipCity	ShipRegion	ShipPostalCode	ShipCountry
10000	LILAS	3	11/16/1994 00:00:00	12/14/1994 00:00:00	11/28/1994 00:00:00	1	12.75	LILA-Supermercado	Carrera 52 con Ave. Bolívar #65-98 Llano Largo	Barquisimeto	Lara	3508	Venezuela
10301	BONAP	6	11/16/1994 00:00:00	12/14/1994 00:00:00	11/21/1994 00:00:00	1	28.89	Bon app'	12, rue des Bouchers	Marseille		13008	France
10302	MEREP	3	11/17/1994 00:00:00	12/26/1994 00:00:00	11/01/1994 00:00:00	1	32.84	Mère Paillarde	43 rue St. Laurent	Montréal	Québec	H1J 1C3	Canada
10303	WARTH	5	11/18/1994 00:00:00	12/16/1994 00:00:00	11/23/1994 00:00:00	3	6.59	Wartian Herkku	Torikatu 38	Oulu		90110	Finland
10304	VICTE	8	11/21/1994 00:00:00	12/16/1994 00:00:00	11/26/1994 00:00:00	2	6.59	Victuailles en stock	2, rue du Commerce	Lyon		69004	France
10305	HUNGO	7	11/22/1994 00:00:00	12/20/1994 00:00:00	11/04/1994 00:00:00	3	42.11	Hungry Owl All-Night Grocers	8 Johnstown Road	Cork	Co. Cork		Ireland
10306	JNUNO	3	11/22/1994 00:00:00	12/11/1994 00:00:00	11/01/1994 00:00:00	3	15.53	Princesa Isabel Vinhos	Estrada da saúde n. 58	Lisboa		1756	Portugal
10307	FRANK	4	11/24/1994 00:00:00	12/22/1994 00:00:00	11/04/1994 00:00:00	3	189.36	Frankenversand	Berliner Platz 43	München		80805	Germany
10308	OLDWO	4	11/25/1994 00:00:00	12/23/1994 00:00:00	11/26/1994 00:00:00	1	84.21	Old World Delicatessen	2743 Bering St.	Anchorage	AK	99508	USA
10309	MEREP	3	11/28/1994 00:00:00	12/26/1994 00:00:00	12/03/1994 00:00:00	2	25.06	Mère Paillarde	43 rue St. Laurent	Montréal	Québec	H1J 1C3	Canada
10340	BONAP	1	11/26/1994 00:00:00	12/27/1994 00:00:00	12/04/1994 00:00:00	3	166.31	Bon app'	12, rue des Bouchers	Marseille		13008	France
10341	SIMOB	7	11/26/1994 00:00:00	12/27/1994 00:00:00	12/06/1994 00:00:00	3	26.78	Simons bistro	Vinbæltet 34	København		1734	Denmark
10342	FRANK	4	11/26/1994 00:00:00	12/05/1994 00:00:00	12/06/1994 00:00:00	2	54.83	Frankenversand	Berliner Platz 43	München		80805	Germany
10343	LEHMS	4	11/27/1994 00:00:00	12/04/1994 00:00:00	12/07/1994 00:00:00	1	110.37	Lehmanns Marktstand	Magazinweg 7	Frankfurt a.M.		60528	Germany
10344	WHITC	4	12/01/1994 00:00:00	12/30/1994 00:00:00	12/06/1994 00:00:00	2	23.29	White Clover Markets	1029 - 12th Ave. S.	Seattle	WA	98124	USA
10345	QUICK	2	12/03/1994 00:00:00	01/03/1995 00:00:00	12/06/1994 00:00:00	2	249.06	QUICK-Stop	Taucherstraße 10	Cunewalde		01307	Germany
10346	RATTC	3	12/06/1994 00:00:00	01/17/1995 00:00:00	12/04/1994 00:00:00	3	142.08	Rattlesnake Canyon Grocery	2817 Milton Dr.	Albuquerque	NM	87110	USA
10348	VINET	3	06/04/1994 00:00:00	09/02/1994 00:00:00	06/16/1994 00:00:00	3	32.38	Vins et alcools Chevalier	59 rue de l'Abbaye	Reims		51100	France
10349	TOMSP	6	08/03/1994 00:00:00	09/16/1994 00:00:00	08/16/1994 00:00:00	1	11.31	Toms Spezialitäten	Luisenstr. 48	Münster		44087	Germany
10350	HANAR	4	08/08/1994 00:00:00	09/05/1994 00:00:00	08/12/1994 00:00:00	2	65.83	Hanari Carnes	Rua do Paço, 67	Rio de Janeiro	RJ	05454-876	Brazil
10351	VICTE	5	08/06/1994 00:00:00	09/03/1994 00:00:00	08/15/1994 00:00:00	1	41.34	Victuailles en stock	2, rue du Commerce	Lyon		69004	France
10352	SUPRD	4	08/09/1994 00:00:00	09/06/1994 00:00:00	08/11/1994 00:00:00	3	31.3	Suprêmes délices	Boulevard Tirou, 255	Charleroi		B-6000	Belgium
10353	HANAR	4	08/16/1994 00:00:00	09/13/1994 00:00:00	08/14/1994 00:00:00	2	58.17	Hanari Carnes	Rua do Paço, 67	Rio de Janeiro	RJ	05454-876	Brazil
10354	CHOPS	3	08/11/1994 00:00:00	09/08/1994 00:00:00	08/13/1994 00:00:00	2	72.38	Chop-suey Chinese	Hauptstr. 31	Bern		3012	Switzerland
10355	GALED	6	08/12/1994 00:00:00	09/09/1994 00:00:00	08/23/1994 00:00:00	3	148.37	Berther Supermkt	Starenweg 5	Genève		1204	Switzerland
10356	WELLI	3	08/13/1994 00:00:00	09/12/1994 00:00:00	08/17/1994 00:00:00	2	13.97	Wellington Importadora	Rua do Mercado, 12	Resende	SP	08737-363	Brazil
10357	HILAA	4	08/16/1994 00:00:00	09/13/1994 00:00:00	08/23/1994 00:00:00	3	81.91	HILARION-Abastos	Carrera 22 con Ave. Carlos Soublette #8-35	San Cristóbal	Táchira	5037	Venezuela
10358	ERNSH	1	08/17/1994 00:00:00	09/14/1994 00:00:00	08/22/1994 00:00:00	1	149.51	Ernst Handel	Kirchgasse 6	Graz		8010	Austria
10359	CENTC	4	08/18/1994 00:00:00	09/11/1994 00:00:00	08/31/1994 00:00:00	3	3.25	Centro comercial Moctezuma	Sierras de Granada 9993	México D.F.		05022	Mexico
10360	OTTIK	4	08/19/1994 00:00:00	09/16/1994 00:00:00	08/26/1994 00:00:00	1	35.06	Ottilies Käseladen	Mehrheimerstr. 369	Köln		50739	Germany
10361	QUEDE	4	08/16/1994 00:00:00	09/16/1994 00:00:00	08/30/1994 00:00:00	2	3.05	Que Delícia	Rua da Panificadora, 12	Rio de Janeiro	RJ	02389-673	Brazil

Table

78

None:

Black and White

Colored:

AccountExpires	AuthorizationFlags	BadPasswordCount	Caption	CodePage	Comment	CountryCode	Description
			NT AUTHORITY\SYSTEM				Network login profile settings for SYSTEM on NT AUTHORITY
			NT AUTHORITY\LOCAL SERVICE				Network login profile settings for LOCAL SERVICE on NT AUTHORITY
			NT AUTHORITY\NETWORK SERVICE				Network login profile settings for NETWORK SERVICE on NT AUTHORITY
	0	0	Administrator	0	Built-in account for administering the computer/domain	0	Network login profile settings for on WIN-S8FLOAK84F9H
			NT SERVICE\S6A3TELEMETRY				Network login profile settings for S6A3TELEMETRY on NT SERVICE
			NT SERVICE\S6S3TELEMETRY130				Network login profile settings for S6S3TELEMETRY130 on NT SERVICE
			NT SERVICE\SQLTELEMETRY				Network login profile settings for SQLTELEMETRY on NT SERVICE
			NT SERVICE\MSSQLServerOLAPService				Network login profile settings for MSSQLServerOLAPService on NT SERVICE
			NT SERVICE\ReportServer				Network login profile settings for ReportServer on NT SERVICE
			NT SERVICE\MSSQLFDLauncher				Network login profile settings for MSSQLFDLauncher on NT SERVICE
			NT SERVICE\MSSQLLaunchpad				Network login profile settings for MSSQLLaunchpad on NT SERVICE
			NT SERVICE\MsDtsServer130				Network login profile settings for MsDtsServer130 on NT SERVICE
			NT SERVICE\MSSQLSERVER				Network login profile settings for MSSQLSERVER on NT SERVICE
			IIS APPPOOL\Classic .NET AppPool				Network login profile settings for Classic .NET AppPool on IIS APPPOOL
			IIS APPPOOL\.NET v4.5				Network login profile settings for .NET v4.5 on IIS APPPOOL
			IIS APPPOOL\.NET v2.0				Network login profile settings for .NET v2.0 on IIS APPPOOL
			IIS APPPOOL\.NET v4.5 Classic				Network login profile settings for .NET v4.5 Classic on IIS APPPOOL
			IIS APPPOOL\.NET v2.0 Classic				Network login profile settings for .NET v2.0 Classic on IIS APPPOOL

Oscillating:

Availability	BytesPerSector	Capabilities	CapabilityDescriptions	Caption	CompressionMethod	ConfigManagerErrorCode	ConfigManagerUserConfig
	512	3, 4, 10	Random Access, Supports Writing, SMART Notification	OCZ REVODRIVE350 SCSI Disk Device		0	FALSE
	512	3, 4	Random Access, Supports Writing	NVMe TOSHIBA-RD400		0	FALSE
	512	3, 4, 10	Random Access, Supports Writing, SMART Notification	TOSHIBA DT01ACA200		0	FALSE

3D:

Availability	BytesPerSector	Capabilities	CapabilityDescriptions	Caption	CompressionMethod	ConfigManagerErrorCode	ConfigManagerUserConfig	CreationClassName
	512	3, 4, 10	Random Access, Supports Writing, SMART Notification	OCZ REVODRIVE350 SCSI Disk Device		0	FALSE	Win32_DiskDrive
	512	3, 4	Random Access, Supports Writing	NVMe TOSHIBA-RD400		0	FALSE	Win32_DiskDrive
	512	3, 4, 10	Random Access, Supports Writing, SMART Notification	TOSHIBA DT01ACA200		0	FALSE	Win32_DiskDrive

Shadow Box:

Availability	BytesPerSector	Capabilities	CapabilityDescriptions	Caption	CompressionMethod	ConfigManagerErrorCode	ConfigManagerUserConfig	CreationClassName	DefaultBlockSize
	512	3, 4, 10	Random Access, Supports Writing, SMART Notification	OCZ REVODRIVE350 SCSI Disk Device		0	FALSE	Win32_DiskDrive	
	512	3, 4	Random Access, Supports Writing	NVMe TOSHIBA-RD400		0	FALSE	Win32_DiskDrive	
	512	3, 4, 10	Random Access, Supports Writing, SMART Notification	TOSHIBA DT01ACA200		0	FALSE	Win32_DiskDrive	

Shadow Box Single Line Vertical

BiosCharacteristics	7, 10, 11, 12, 15, 16, 17, 19, 23, 24, 25, 26, 27, 28, 29, 32, 33, 40, 42, 43, 48, 50, 58, 59, 64, 65, 66, 67, 68, 69, 70, 71, 72, 73, 74, 75, 76, 77, 78, 79
BIOSVersion	ALASKA - 1072009, 0504, American Megatrends - 5000C
BuildNumber	
Caption	0504
CodeSet	
CurrentLanguage	en|US|iso8859-1
Description	0504
IdentificationCode	
InstallableLanguages	8
InstallDate	
LanguageEdition	
ListOfLanguages	en|US|iso8859-1, fr|FR|iso8859-1, zh|CN|unicode, , , ,
Manufacturer	American Megatrends Inc.
Name	0504
OtherTargetOS	
PrimaryBIOS	TRUE

Shadow Box Multi line Vertical

Availability			
BytesPerSector	512	512	512
Capabilities	3, 4, 10	3, 4	3, 4, 10
CapabilityDescriptions	Random Access, Supports Writing, SMART Notification	Random Access, Supports Writing	Random Access, Supports Writing, SMART Notification
Caption	OCZ REVODRIVE350 SCSI Disk Device	NVMe TOSHIBA-RD400	TOSHIBA DT01ACA200
CompressionMethod			
ConfigManagerErrorCode	0	0	0
ConfigManagerUserConfig	FALSE	FALSE	FALSE
CreationClassName	Win32_DiskDrive	Win32_DiskDrive	Win32_DiskDrive
DefaultBlockSize			
Description	Disk drive	Disk drive	Disk drive
DeviceID	\\.\PHYSICALDRIVE2	\\.\PHYSICALDRIVE1	\\.\PHYSICALDRIVE0
ErrorCleared			
ErrorDescription			
ErrorMethodology			
FirmwareRevision	2.50	57CZ4102	MX4OAR00
Index	2	1	0

STYLESHEETS CODE

Decorating your web pages

BELOW ARE SOME STYLESHEETS I COOKED UP THAT I LIKE AND THINK YOU MIGHT TOO. Don't worry I won't be offended if you take and modify to your hearts delight. Please do!

NONE

```
txtstream.WriteLine("<style type='text/css'>")
txtstream.WriteLine("th")
txtstream.WriteLine("{")
txtstream.WriteLine("    COLOR: darkred;")
txtstream.WriteLine("}")
txtstream.WriteLine("td")
txtstream.WriteLine("{")
txtstream.WriteLine("    COLOR: Navy;")
txtstream.WriteLine("}")
txtstream.WriteLine("</style>")
```

BLACK AND WHITE TEXT

```
txtstream.WriteLine("<style type='text/css'>")
txtstream.WriteLine("th")
txtstream.WriteLine("{")
```

```
txtstream.WriteLine("    COLOR: white;")
txtstream.WriteLine("    BACKGROUND-COLOR: black;")
txtstream.WriteLine("    FONT-FAMILY:font-family: Cambria, serif;")
txtstream.WriteLine("    FONT-SIZE: 12px;")
txtstream.WriteLine("    text-align: left;")
txtstream.WriteLine("    white-Space: nowrap;")
txtstream.WriteLine("}")
txtstream.WriteLine("td")
txtstream.WriteLine("{")
txtstream.WriteLine("    COLOR: white;")
txtstream.WriteLine("    BACKGROUND-COLOR: black;")
txtstream.WriteLine("    FONT-FAMILY: font-family: Cambria, serif;")
txtstream.WriteLine("    FONT-SIZE: 12px;")
txtstream.WriteLine("    text-align: left;")
txtstream.WriteLine("    white-Space: nowrap;")
txtstream.WriteLine("}")
txtstream.WriteLine("div")
txtstream.WriteLine("{")
txtstream.WriteLine("    COLOR: white;")
txtstream.WriteLine("    BACKGROUND-COLOR: black;")
txtstream.WriteLine("    FONT-FAMILY: font-family: Cambria, serif;")
txtstream.WriteLine("    FONT-SIZE: 10px;")
txtstream.WriteLine("    text-align: left;")
txtstream.WriteLine("    white-Space: nowrap;")
txtstream.WriteLine("}")
txtstream.WriteLine("span")
txtstream.WriteLine("{")
txtstream.WriteLine("    COLOR: white;")
txtstream.WriteLine("    BACKGROUND-COLOR: black;")
txtstream.WriteLine("    FONT-FAMILY: font-family: Cambria, serif;")
txtstream.WriteLine("    FONT-SIZE: 10px;")
txtstream.WriteLine("    text-align: left;")
txtstream.WriteLine("    white-Space: nowrap;")
```

```
txtstream.WriteLine("    display:inline-block;")
txtstream.WriteLine("    width: 100%;")
txtstream.WriteLine("}")
txtstream.WriteLine("textarea")
txtstream.WriteLine("{")
txtstream.WriteLine("    COLOR: white;")
txtstream.WriteLine("    BACKGROUND-COLOR: black;")
txtstream.WriteLine("    FONT-FAMILY: font-family: Cambria, serif;")
txtstream.WriteLine("    FONT-SIZE: 10px;")
txtstream.WriteLine("    text-align: left;")
txtstream.WriteLine("    white-Space: nowrap;")
txtstream.WriteLine("    width: 100%;")
txtstream.WriteLine("}")
txtstream.WriteLine("select")
txtstream.WriteLine("{")
txtstream.WriteLine("    COLOR: white;")
txtstream.WriteLine("    BACKGROUND-COLOR: black;")
txtstream.WriteLine("    FONT-FAMILY: font-family: Cambria, serif;")
txtstream.WriteLine("    FONT-SIZE: 10px;")
txtstream.WriteLine("    text-align: left;")
txtstream.WriteLine("    white-Space: nowrap;")
txtstream.WriteLine("    width: 100%;")
txtstream.WriteLine("}")
txtstream.WriteLine("input")
txtstream.WriteLine("{")
txtstream.WriteLine("    COLOR: white;")
txtstream.WriteLine("    BACKGROUND-COLOR: black;")
txtstream.WriteLine("    FONT-FAMILY: font-family: Cambria, serif;")
txtstream.WriteLine("    FONT-SIZE: 12px;")
txtstream.WriteLine("    text-align: left;")
txtstream.WriteLine("    display:table-cell;")
txtstream.WriteLine("    white-Space: nowrap;")
txtstream.WriteLine("}")
```

```
txtstream.WriteLine("h1 {")
txtstream.WriteLine("color: antiquewhite;")
txtstream.WriteLine("text-shadow: 1px 1px 1px black;")
txtstream.WriteLine("padding: 3px;")
txtstream.WriteLine("text-align: center;")
txtstream.WriteLine("box-shadow: inset 2px 2px 5px rgba(0,0,0,0.5), inset -2px -2px 5px rgba(255,255,255,0.5)")
txtstream.WriteLine("}")
txtstream.WriteLine("</style>")
```

COLORED TEXT

```
txtstream.WriteLine("<style type='text/css'>")
txtstream.WriteLine("th")
txtstream.WriteLine("{")
txtstream.WriteLine("    COLOR: darkred;")
txtstream.WriteLine("    BACKGROUND-COLOR: #eeeeee;")
txtstream.WriteLine("    FONT-FAMILY:font-family: Cambria, serif;")
txtstream.WriteLine("    FONT-SIZE: 12px;")
txtstream.WriteLine("    text-align: left;")
txtstream.WriteLine("    white-Space: nowrap;")
txtstream.WriteLine("}")
txtstream.WriteLine("td")
txtstream.WriteLine("{")
txtstream.WriteLine("    COLOR: navy;")
txtstream.WriteLine("    BACKGROUND-COLOR: #eeeeee;")
txtstream.WriteLine("    FONT-FAMILY: font-family: Cambria, serif;")
txtstream.WriteLine("    FONT-SIZE: 12px;")
txtstream.WriteLine("    text-align: left;")
txtstream.WriteLine("    white-Space: nowrap;")
txtstream.WriteLine("}")
txtstream.WriteLine("div")
txtstream.WriteLine("{")
```

```
txtstream.WriteLine("   COLOR: white;")
txtstream.WriteLine("   BACKGROUND-COLOR: navy;")
txtstream.WriteLine("   FONT-FAMILY: font-family: Cambria, serif;")
txtstream.WriteLine("   FONT-SIZE: 10px;")
txtstream.WriteLine("   text-align: left;")
txtstream.WriteLine("   white-Space: nowrap;")
txtstream.WriteLine("}")
txtstream.WriteLine("span")
txtstream.WriteLine("{")
txtstream.WriteLine("   COLOR: white;")
txtstream.WriteLine("   BACKGROUND-COLOR: navy;")
txtstream.WriteLine("   FONT-FAMILY: font-family: Cambria, serif;")
txtstream.WriteLine("   FONT-SIZE: 10px;")
txtstream.WriteLine("   text-align: left;")
txtstream.WriteLine("   white-Space: nowrap;")
txtstream.WriteLine("   display:inline-block;")
txtstream.WriteLine("   width: 100%;")
txtstream.WriteLine("}")
txtstream.WriteLine("textarea")
txtstream.WriteLine("{")
txtstream.WriteLine("   COLOR: white;")
txtstream.WriteLine("   BACKGROUND-COLOR: navy;")
txtstream.WriteLine("   FONT-FAMILY: font-family: Cambria, serif;")
txtstream.WriteLine("   FONT-SIZE: 10px;")
txtstream.WriteLine("   text-align: left;")
txtstream.WriteLine("   white-Space: nowrap;")
txtstream.WriteLine("   width: 100%;")
txtstream.WriteLine("}")
txtstream.WriteLine("select")
txtstream.WriteLine("{")
txtstream.WriteLine("   COLOR: white;")
txtstream.WriteLine("   BACKGROUND-COLOR: navy;")
txtstream.WriteLine("   FONT-FAMILY: font-family: Cambria, serif;")
```

```
txtstream.WriteLine("    FONT-SIZE: 10px;")
txtstream.WriteLine("    text-align: left;")
txtstream.WriteLine("    white-Space: nowrap;")
txtstream.WriteLine("    width: 100%;")
txtstream.WriteLine("}")
txtstream.WriteLine("input")
txtstream.WriteLine("{")
txtstream.WriteLine("    COLOR: white;")
txtstream.WriteLine("    BACKGROUND-COLOR: navy;")
txtstream.WriteLine("    FONT-FAMILY: font-family: Cambria, serif;")
txtstream.WriteLine("    FONT-SIZE: 12px;")
txtstream.WriteLine("    text-align: left;")
txtstream.WriteLine("    display:table-cell;")
txtstream.WriteLine("    white-Space: nowrap;")
txtstream.WriteLine("}")
txtstream.WriteLine("h1 {")
txtstream.WriteLine("color: antiquewhite;")
txtstream.WriteLine("text-shadow: 1px 1px 1px black;")
txtstream.WriteLine("padding: 3px;")
txtstream.WriteLine("text-align: center;")
txtstream.WriteLine("box-shadow: inset 2px 2px 5px rgba(0,0,0,0.5), inset -
2px -2px 5px rgba(255,255,255,0.5)")
txtstream.WriteLine("}")
txtstream.WriteLine("</style>")
```

OSCILLATING ROW COLORS

```
txtstream.WriteLine("<style>")
txtstream.WriteLine("th")
txtstream.WriteLine("{")
txtstream.WriteLine("    COLOR: white;")
```

```
txtstream.WriteLine("    BACKGROUND-COLOR: navy;")
txtstream.WriteLine("    FONT-FAMILY:font-family: Cambria, serif;")
txtstream.WriteLine("    FONT-SIZE: 12px;")
txtstream.WriteLine("    text-align: left;")
txtstream.WriteLine("    white-Space: nowrap;")
txtstream.WriteLine("}")
txtstream.WriteLine("td")
txtstream.WriteLine("{")
txtstream.WriteLine("    COLOR: navy;")
txtstream.WriteLine("    FONT-FAMILY: font-family: Cambria, serif;")
txtstream.WriteLine("    FONT-SIZE: 12px;")
txtstream.WriteLine("    text-align: left;")
txtstream.WriteLine("    white-Space: nowrap;")
txtstream.WriteLine("}")
txtstream.WriteLine("div")
txtstream.WriteLine("{")
txtstream.WriteLine("    COLOR: navy;")
txtstream.WriteLine("    FONT-FAMILY: font-family: Cambria, serif;")
txtstream.WriteLine("    FONT-SIZE: 12px;")
txtstream.WriteLine("    text-align: left;")
txtstream.WriteLine("    white-Space: nowrap;")
txtstream.WriteLine("}")
txtstream.WriteLine("span")
txtstream.WriteLine("{")
txtstream.WriteLine("    COLOR: navy;")
txtstream.WriteLine("    FONT-FAMILY: font-family: Cambria, serif;")
txtstream.WriteLine("    FONT-SIZE: 12px;")
txtstream.WriteLine("    text-align: left;")
txtstream.WriteLine("    white-Space: nowrap;")
txtstream.WriteLine("    width: 100%;")
txtstream.WriteLine("}")
txtstream.WriteLine("textarea")
txtstream.WriteLine("{")
```

```
txtstream.WriteLine("    COLOR: navy;")
txtstream.WriteLine("    FONT-FAMILY: font-family: Cambria, serif;")
txtstream.WriteLine("    FONT-SIZE: 12px;")
txtstream.WriteLine("    text-align: left;")
txtstream.WriteLine("    white-Space: nowrap;")
txtstream.WriteLine("    display:inline-block;")
txtstream.WriteLine("    width: 100%;")
txtstream.WriteLine("}")
txtstream.WriteLine("select")
txtstream.WriteLine("{")
txtstream.WriteLine("    COLOR: navy;")
txtstream.WriteLine("    FONT-FAMILY: font-family: Cambria, serif;")
txtstream.WriteLine("    FONT-SIZE: 10px;")
txtstream.WriteLine("    text-align: left;")
txtstream.WriteLine("    white-Space: nowrap;")
txtstream.WriteLine("    display:inline-block;")
txtstream.WriteLine("    width: 100%;")
txtstream.WriteLine("}")
txtstream.WriteLine("input")
txtstream.WriteLine("{")
txtstream.WriteLine("    COLOR: navy;")
txtstream.WriteLine("    FONT-FAMILY: font-family: Cambria, serif;")
txtstream.WriteLine("    FONT-SIZE: 12px;")
txtstream.WriteLine("    text-align: left;")
txtstream.WriteLine("    display:table-cell;")
txtstream.WriteLine("    white-Space: nowrap;")
txtstream.WriteLine("}")
txtstream.WriteLine("h1 {")
txtstream.WriteLine("color: antiquewhite;")
txtstream.WriteLine("text-shadow: 1px 1px 1px black;")
txtstream.WriteLine("padding: 3px;")
txtstream.WriteLine("text-align: center;")
```

```
txtstream.WriteLine("box-shadow: inset 2px 2px 5px rgba(0,0,0,0.5), inset -
2px -2px 5px rgba(255,255,255,0.5)")
txtstream.WriteLine("}")
txtstream.WriteLine("tr:nth-child(even){background-color:#f2f2f2;}")
txtstream.WriteLine("tr:nth-child(odd){background-color:#cccccc;
color:#f2f2f2;}")
txtstream.WriteLine("</style>")
```

GHOST DECORATED

```
txtstream.WriteLine("<style type='text/css'>")
txtstream.WriteLine("th")
txtstream.WriteLine("{")
txtstream.WriteLine("   COLOR: black;")
txtstream.WriteLine("   BACKGROUND-COLOR: white;")
txtstream.WriteLine("   FONT-FAMILY:font-family: Cambria, serif;")
txtstream.WriteLine("   FONT-SIZE: 12px;")
txtstream.WriteLine("   text-align: left;")
txtstream.WriteLine("   white-Space: nowrap;")
txtstream.WriteLine("}")
txtstream.WriteLine("td")
txtstream.WriteLine("{")
txtstream.WriteLine("   COLOR: black;")
txtstream.WriteLine("   BACKGROUND-COLOR: white;")
txtstream.WriteLine("   FONT-FAMILY: font-family: Cambria, serif;")
txtstream.WriteLine("   FONT-SIZE: 12px;")
txtstream.WriteLine("   text-align: left;")
txtstream.WriteLine("   white-Space: nowrap;")
txtstream.WriteLine("}")
txtstream.WriteLine("div")
txtstream.WriteLine("{")
txtstream.WriteLine("   COLOR: black;")
txtstream.WriteLine("   BACKGROUND-COLOR: white;")
```

```
txtstream.WriteLine("    FONT-FAMILY: font-family: Cambria, serif;")
txtstream.WriteLine("    FONT-SIZE: 10px;")
txtstream.WriteLine("    text-align: left;")
txtstream.WriteLine("    white-Space: nowrap;")
txtstream.WriteLine("}")
txtstream.WriteLine("span")
txtstream.WriteLine("{")
txtstream.WriteLine("    COLOR: black;")
txtstream.WriteLine("    BACKGROUND-COLOR: white;")
txtstream.WriteLine("    FONT-FAMILY: font-family: Cambria, serif;")
txtstream.WriteLine("    FONT-SIZE: 10px;")
txtstream.WriteLine("    text-align: left;")
txtstream.WriteLine("    white-Space: nowrap;")
txtstream.WriteLine("    display:inline-block;")
txtstream.WriteLine("    width: 100%;")
txtstream.WriteLine("}")
txtstream.WriteLine("textarea")
txtstream.WriteLine("{")
txtstream.WriteLine("    COLOR: black;")
txtstream.WriteLine("    BACKGROUND-COLOR: white;")
txtstream.WriteLine("    FONT-FAMILY: font-family: Cambria, serif;")
txtstream.WriteLine("    FONT-SIZE: 10px;")
txtstream.WriteLine("    text-align: left;")
txtstream.WriteLine("    white-Space: nowrap;")
txtstream.WriteLine("    width: 100%;")
txtstream.WriteLine("}")
txtstream.WriteLine("select")
txtstream.WriteLine("{")
txtstream.WriteLine("    COLOR: black;")
txtstream.WriteLine("    BACKGROUND-COLOR: white;")
txtstream.WriteLine("    FONT-FAMILY: font-family: Cambria, serif;")
txtstream.WriteLine("    FONT-SIZE: 10px;")
txtstream.WriteLine("    text-align: left;")
```

```
txtstream.WriteLine("    white-Space: nowrap;")
txtstream.WriteLine("    width: 100%;")
txtstream.WriteLine("}")
txtstream.WriteLine("input")
txtstream.WriteLine("{")
txtstream.WriteLine("    COLOR: black;")
txtstream.WriteLine("    BACKGROUND-COLOR: white;")
txtstream.WriteLine("    FONT-FAMILY: font-family: Cambria, serif;")
txtstream.WriteLine("    FONT-SIZE: 12px;")
txtstream.WriteLine("    text-align: left;")
txtstream.WriteLine("    display:table-cell;")
txtstream.WriteLine("    white-Space: nowrap;")
txtstream.WriteLine("}")
txtstream.WriteLine("h1 {")
txtstream.WriteLine("color: antiquewhite;")
txtstream.WriteLine("text-shadow: 1px 1px 1px black;")
txtstream.WriteLine("padding: 3px;")
txtstream.WriteLine("text-align: center;")
txtstream.WriteLine("box-shadow: inset 2px 2px 5px rgba(0,0,0,0.5), inset -
2px -2px 5px rgba(255,255,255,0.5)")
txtstream.WriteLine("}")
txtstream.WriteLine("</style>")


3D


txtstream.WriteLine("<style type='text/css'>")
txtstream.WriteLine("body")
txtstream.WriteLine("{")
txtstream.WriteLine("    PADDING-RIGHT: 0px;")
txtstream.WriteLine("    PADDING-LEFT: 0px;")
txtstream.WriteLine("    PADDING-BOTTOM: 0px;")
txtstream.WriteLine("    MARGIN: 0px;")
```

```
txtstream.WriteLine("    COLOR: #333;")
txtstream.WriteLine("    PADDING-TOP: 0px;")
txtstream.WriteLine("    FONT-FAMILY: verdana, arial, helvetica, sans-serif;")
txtstream.WriteLine("}")
txtstream.WriteLine("table")
txtstream.WriteLine("{“)
txtstream.WriteLine("    BORDER-RIGHT: #999999 3px solid;")
txtstream.WriteLine("    PADDING-RIGHT: 6px;")
txtstream.WriteLine("    PADDING-LEFT: 6px;")
txtstream.WriteLine("    FONT-WEIGHT: Bold;")
txtstream.WriteLine("    FONT-SIZE: 14px;")
txtstream.WriteLine("    PADDING-BOTTOM: 6px;")
txtstream.WriteLine("    COLOR: Peru;")
txtstream.WriteLine("    LINE-HEIGHT: 14px;")
txtstream.WriteLine("    PADDING-TOP: 6px;")
txtstream.WriteLine("    BORDER-BOTTOM: #999 1px solid;")
txtstream.WriteLine("    BACKGROUND-COLOR: #eeeeee;")
txtstream.WriteLine("    FONT-FAMILY: verdana, arial, helvetica, sans-serif;")
txtstream.WriteLine("    FONT-SIZE: 12px;")
txtstream.WriteLine("}")
txtstream.WriteLine("th")
txtstream.WriteLine("{“)
txtstream.WriteLine("    BORDER-RIGHT: #999999 3px solid;")
txtstream.WriteLine("    PADDING-RIGHT: 6px;")
txtstream.WriteLine("    PADDING-LEFT: 6px;")
txtstream.WriteLine("    FONT-WEIGHT: Bold;")
txtstream.WriteLine("    FONT-SIZE: 14px;")
txtstream.WriteLine("    PADDING-BOTTOM: 6px;")
txtstream.WriteLine("    COLOR: darkred;")
txtstream.WriteLine("    LINE-HEIGHT: 14px;")
txtstream.WriteLine("    PADDING-TOP: 6px;")
txtstream.WriteLine("    BORDER-BOTTOM: #999 1px solid;")
txtstream.WriteLine("    BACKGROUND-COLOR: #eeeeee;")
```

```
txtstream.WriteLine("   FONT-FAMILY:font-family: Cambria, serif;")
txtstream.WriteLine("   FONT-SIZE: 12px;")
txtstream.WriteLine("   text-align: left;")
txtstream.WriteLine("   white-Space: nowrap;")
txtstream.WriteLine("}")
txtstream.WriteLine(".th")
txtstream.WriteLine("{")
txtstream.WriteLine("   BORDER-RIGHT: #999999 2px solid;")
txtstream.WriteLine("   PADDING-RIGHT: 6px;")
txtstream.WriteLine("   PADDING-LEFT: 6px;")
txtstream.WriteLine("   FONT-WEIGHT: Bold;")
txtstream.WriteLine("   PADDING-BOTTOM: 6px;")
txtstream.WriteLine("   COLOR: black;")
txtstream.WriteLine("   PADDING-TOP: 6px;")
txtstream.WriteLine("   BORDER-BOTTOM: #999 2px solid;")
txtstream.WriteLine("   BACKGROUND-COLOR: #eeeeee;")
txtstream.WriteLine("   FONT-FAMILY: font-family: Cambria, serif;")
txtstream.WriteLine("   FONT-SIZE: 10px;")
txtstream.WriteLine("   text-align: right;")
txtstream.WriteLine("   white-Space: nowrap;")
txtstream.WriteLine("}")
txtstream.WriteLine("td")
txtstream.WriteLine("{")
txtstream.WriteLine("   BORDER-RIGHT: #999999 3px solid;")
txtstream.WriteLine("   PADDING-RIGHT: 6px;")
txtstream.WriteLine("   PADDING-LEFT: 6px;")
txtstream.WriteLine("   FONT-WEIGHT: Normal;")
txtstream.WriteLine("   PADDING-BOTTOM: 6px;")
txtstream.WriteLine("   COLOR: navy;")
txtstream.WriteLine("   LINE-HEIGHT: 14px;")
txtstream.WriteLine("   PADDING-TOP: 6px;")
txtstream.WriteLine("   BORDER-BOTTOM: #999 1px solid;")
txtstream.WriteLine("   BACKGROUND-COLOR: #eeeeee;")
```

```
txtstream.WriteLine("    FONT-FAMILY: font-family: Cambria, serif;")
txtstream.WriteLine("    FONT-SIZE: 12px;")
txtstream.WriteLine("    text-align: left;")
txtstream.WriteLine("    white-Space: nowrap;")
txtstream.WriteLine("}")
txtstream.WriteLine("div")
txtstream.WriteLine("{")
txtstream.WriteLine("    BORDER-RIGHT: #999999 3px solid;")
txtstream.WriteLine("    PADDING-RIGHT: 6px;")
txtstream.WriteLine("    PADDING-LEFT: 6px;")
txtstream.WriteLine("    FONT-WEIGHT: Normal;")
txtstream.WriteLine("    PADDING-BOTTOM: 6px;")
txtstream.WriteLine("    COLOR: white;")
txtstream.WriteLine("    PADDING-TOP: 6px;")
txtstream.WriteLine("    BORDER-BOTTOM: #999 1px solid;")
txtstream.WriteLine("    BACKGROUND-COLOR: navy;")
txtstream.WriteLine("    FONT-FAMILY: font-family: Cambria, serif;")
txtstream.WriteLine("    FONT-SIZE: 10px;")
txtstream.WriteLine("    text-align: left;")
txtstream.WriteLine("    white-Space: nowrap;")
txtstream.WriteLine("}")
txtstream.WriteLine("span")
txtstream.WriteLine("{")
txtstream.WriteLine("    BORDER-RIGHT: #999999 3px solid;")
txtstream.WriteLine("    PADDING-RIGHT: 3px;")
txtstream.WriteLine("    PADDING-LEFT: 3px;")
txtstream.WriteLine("    FONT-WEIGHT: Normal;")
txtstream.WriteLine("    PADDING-BOTTOM: 3px;")
txtstream.WriteLine("    COLOR: white;")
txtstream.WriteLine("    PADDING-TOP: 3px;")
txtstream.WriteLine("    BORDER-BOTTOM: #999 1px solid;")
txtstream.WriteLine("    BACKGROUND-COLOR: navy;")
txtstream.WriteLine("    FONT-FAMILY: font-family: Cambria, serif;")
```

```
txtstream.WriteLine("    FONT-SIZE: 10px;")
txtstream.WriteLine("    text-align: left;")
txtstream.WriteLine("    white-Space: nowrap;")
txtstream.WriteLine("    display:inline-block;")
txtstream.WriteLine("    width: 100%;")
txtstream.WriteLine("}")
txtstream.WriteLine("textarea")
txtstream.WriteLine("{")
txtstream.WriteLine("    BORDER-RIGHT: #999999 3px solid;")
txtstream.WriteLine("    PADDING-RIGHT: 3px;")
txtstream.WriteLine("    PADDING-LEFT: 3px;")
txtstream.WriteLine("    FONT-WEIGHT: Normal;")
txtstream.WriteLine("    PADDING-BOTTOM: 3px;")
txtstream.WriteLine("    COLOR: white;")
txtstream.WriteLine("    PADDING-TOP: 3px;")
txtstream.WriteLine("    BORDER-BOTTOM: #999 1px solid;")
txtstream.WriteLine("    BACKGROUND-COLOR: navy;")
txtstream.WriteLine("    FONT-FAMILY: font-family: Cambria, serif;")
txtstream.WriteLine("    FONT-SIZE: 10px;")
txtstream.WriteLine("    text-align: left;")
txtstream.WriteLine("    white-Space: nowrap;")
txtstream.WriteLine("    width: 100%;")
txtstream.WriteLine("}")
txtstream.WriteLine("select")
txtstream.WriteLine("{")
txtstream.WriteLine("    BORDER-RIGHT: #999999 3px solid;")
txtstream.WriteLine("    PADDING-RIGHT: 6px;")
txtstream.WriteLine("    PADDING-LEFT: 6px;")
txtstream.WriteLine("    FONT-WEIGHT: Normal;")
txtstream.WriteLine("    PADDING-BOTTOM: 6px;")
txtstream.WriteLine("    COLOR: white;")
txtstream.WriteLine("    PADDING-TOP: 6px;")
txtstream.WriteLine("    BORDER-BOTTOM: #999 1px solid;")
```

```
txtstream.WriteLine("    BACKGROUND-COLOR: navy;")
txtstream.WriteLine("    FONT-FAMILY: font-family: Cambria, serif;")
txtstream.WriteLine("    FONT-SIZE: 10px;")
txtstream.WriteLine("    text-align: left;")
txtstream.WriteLine("    white-Space: nowrap;")
txtstream.WriteLine("    width: 100%;")
txtstream.WriteLine("}")
txtstream.WriteLine("input")
txtstream.WriteLine("{")
txtstream.WriteLine("    BORDER-RIGHT: #999999 3px solid;")
txtstream.WriteLine("    PADDING-RIGHT: 3px;")
txtstream.WriteLine("    PADDING-LEFT: 3px;")
txtstream.WriteLine("    FONT-WEIGHT: Bold;")
txtstream.WriteLine("    PADDING-BOTTOM: 3px;")
txtstream.WriteLine("    COLOR: white;")
txtstream.WriteLine("    PADDING-TOP: 3px;")
txtstream.WriteLine("    BORDER-BOTTOM: #999 1px solid;")
txtstream.WriteLine("    BACKGROUND-COLOR: navy;")
txtstream.WriteLine("    FONT-FAMILY: font-family: Cambria, serif;")
txtstream.WriteLine("    FONT-SIZE: 12px;")
txtstream.WriteLine("    text-align: left;")
txtstream.WriteLine("    display:table-cell;")
txtstream.WriteLine("    white-Space: nowrap;")
txtstream.WriteLine("    width: 100%;")
txtstream.WriteLine("}")
txtstream.WriteLine("h1 {")
txtstream.WriteLine("color: antiquewhite;")
txtstream.WriteLine("text-shadow: 1px 1px 1px black;")
txtstream.WriteLine("padding: 3px;")
txtstream.WriteLine("text-align: center;")
txtstream.WriteLine("box-shadow: inset 2px 2px 5px rgba(0,0,0,0.5), inset -2px -2px 5px rgba(255,255,255,0.5)")
txtstream.WriteLine("}")
```

```
txtstream.WriteLine("</style>")
```

SHADOW BOX

```
txtstream.WriteLine("<style type='text/css'>")
txtstream.WriteLine("body")
txtstream.WriteLine("{")
txtstream.WriteLine("   PADDING-RIGHT: 0px;")
txtstream.WriteLine("   PADDING-LEFT: 0px;")
txtstream.WriteLine("   PADDING-BOTTOM: 0px;")
txtstream.WriteLine("   MARGIN: 0px;")
txtstream.WriteLine("   COLOR: #333;")
txtstream.WriteLine("   PADDING-TOP: 0px;")
txtstream.WriteLine("   FONT-FAMILY: verdana, arial, helvetica, sans-serif;")
txtstream.WriteLine("}")
txtstream.WriteLine("table")
txtstream.WriteLine("{")
txtstream.WriteLine("   BORDER-RIGHT: #999999 1px solid;")
txtstream.WriteLine("   PADDING-RIGHT: 1px;")
txtstream.WriteLine("   PADDING-LEFT: 1px;")
txtstream.WriteLine("   PADDING-BOTTOM: 1px;")
txtstream.WriteLine("   LINE-HEIGHT: 8px;")
txtstream.WriteLine("   PADDING-TOP: 1px;")
txtstream.WriteLine("   BORDER-BOTTOM: #999 1px solid;")
txtstream.WriteLine("   BACKGROUND-COLOR: #eeeeee;")
txtstream.WriteLine("
filter:progid:DXImageTransform.Microsoft.Shadow(color='silver',     Direction=135,
Strength=16)")
txtstream.WriteLine("}")
txtstream.WriteLine("th")
txtstream.WriteLine("{")
txtstream.WriteLine("   BORDER-RIGHT: #999999 3px solid;")
txtstream.WriteLine("   PADDING-RIGHT: 6px;")
```

```
txtstream.WriteLine("    PADDING-LEFT: 6px;")
txtstream.WriteLine("    FONT-WEIGHT: Bold;")
txtstream.WriteLine("    FONT-SIZE: 14px;")
txtstream.WriteLine("    PADDING-BOTTOM: 6px;")
txtstream.WriteLine("    COLOR: darkred;")
txtstream.WriteLine("    LINE-HEIGHT: 14px;")
txtstream.WriteLine("    PADDING-TOP: 6px;")
txtstream.WriteLine("    BORDER-BOTTOM: #999 1px solid;")
txtstream.WriteLine("    BACKGROUND-COLOR: #eeeeee;")
txtstream.WriteLine("    FONT-FAMILY: font-family: Cambria, serif;")
txtstream.WriteLine("    FONT-SIZE: 12px;")
txtstream.WriteLine("    text-align: left;")
txtstream.WriteLine("    white-Space: nowrap;")
txtstream.WriteLine("}")
txtstream.WriteLine(".th")
txtstream.WriteLine("{")
txtstream.WriteLine("    BORDER-RIGHT: #999999 2px solid;")
txtstream.WriteLine("    PADDING-RIGHT: 6px;")
txtstream.WriteLine("    PADDING-LEFT: 6px;")
txtstream.WriteLine("    FONT-WEIGHT: Bold;")
txtstream.WriteLine("    PADDING-BOTTOM: 6px;")
txtstream.WriteLine("    COLOR: black;")
txtstream.WriteLine("    PADDING-TOP: 6px;")
txtstream.WriteLine("    BORDER-BOTTOM: #999 2px solid;")
txtstream.WriteLine("    BACKGROUND-COLOR: #eeeeee;")
txtstream.WriteLine("    FONT-FAMILY: font-family: Cambria, serif;")
txtstream.WriteLine("    FONT-SIZE: 10px;")
txtstream.WriteLine("    text-align: right;")
txtstream.WriteLine("    white-Space: nowrap;")
txtstream.WriteLine("}")
txtstream.WriteLine("td")
txtstream.WriteLine("{")
txtstream.WriteLine("    BORDER-RIGHT: #999999 3px solid;")
```

```
txtstream.WriteLine("    PADDING-RIGHT: 6px;")
txtstream.WriteLine("    PADDING-LEFT: 6px;")
txtstream.WriteLine("    FONT-WEIGHT: Normal;")
txtstream.WriteLine("    PADDING-BOTTOM: 6px;")
txtstream.WriteLine("    COLOR: navy;")
txtstream.WriteLine("    LINE-HEIGHT: 14px;")
txtstream.WriteLine("    PADDING-TOP: 6px;")
txtstream.WriteLine("    BORDER-BOTTOM: #999 1px solid;")
txtstream.WriteLine("    BACKGROUND-COLOR: #eeeeee;")
txtstream.WriteLine("    FONT-FAMILY: font-family: Cambria, serif;")
txtstream.WriteLine("    FONT-SIZE: 12px;")
txtstream.WriteLine("    text-align: left;")
txtstream.WriteLine("    white-Space: nowrap;")
txtstream.WriteLine("}")
txtstream.WriteLine("div")
txtstream.WriteLine("{")
txtstream.WriteLine("    BORDER-RIGHT: #999999 3px solid;")
txtstream.WriteLine("    PADDING-RIGHT: 6px;")
txtstream.WriteLine("    PADDING-LEFT: 6px;")
txtstream.WriteLine("    FONT-WEIGHT: Normal;")
txtstream.WriteLine("    PADDING-BOTTOM: 6px;")
txtstream.WriteLine("    COLOR: white;")
txtstream.WriteLine("    PADDING-TOP: 6px;")
txtstream.WriteLine("    BORDER-BOTTOM: #999 1px solid;")
txtstream.WriteLine("    BACKGROUND-COLOR: navy;")
txtstream.WriteLine("    FONT-FAMILY: font-family: Cambria, serif;")
txtstream.WriteLine("    FONT-SIZE: 10px;")
txtstream.WriteLine("    text-align: left;")
txtstream.WriteLine("    white-Space: nowrap;")
txtstream.WriteLine("}")
txtstream.WriteLine("span")
txtstream.WriteLine("{")
txtstream.WriteLine("    BORDER-RIGHT: #999999 3px solid;")
```

```
txtstream.WriteLine("    PADDING-RIGHT: 3px;")
txtstream.WriteLine("    PADDING-LEFT: 3px;")
txtstream.WriteLine("    FONT-WEIGHT: Normal;")
txtstream.WriteLine("    PADDING-BOTTOM: 3px;")
txtstream.WriteLine("    COLOR: white;")
txtstream.WriteLine("    PADDING-TOP: 3px;")
txtstream.WriteLine("    BORDER-BOTTOM: #999 1px solid;")
txtstream.WriteLine("    BACKGROUND-COLOR: navy;")
txtstream.WriteLine("    FONT-FAMILY: font-family: Cambria, serif;")
txtstream.WriteLine("    FONT-SIZE: 10px;")
txtstream.WriteLine("    text-align: left;")
txtstream.WriteLine("    white-Space: nowrap;")
txtstream.WriteLine("    display: inline-block;")
txtstream.WriteLine("    width: 100%;")
txtstream.WriteLine("}")
txtstream.WriteLine("textarea")
txtstream.WriteLine("{")
txtstream.WriteLine("    BORDER-RIGHT: #999999 3px solid;")
txtstream.WriteLine("    PADDING-RIGHT: 3px;")
txtstream.WriteLine("    PADDING-LEFT: 3px;")
txtstream.WriteLine("    FONT-WEIGHT: Normal;")
txtstream.WriteLine("    PADDING-BOTTOM: 3px;")
txtstream.WriteLine("    COLOR: white;")
txtstream.WriteLine("    PADDING-TOP: 3px;")
txtstream.WriteLine("    BORDER-BOTTOM: #999 1px solid;")
txtstream.WriteLine("    BACKGROUND-COLOR: navy;")
txtstream.WriteLine("    FONT-FAMILY: font-family: Cambria, serif;")
txtstream.WriteLine("    FONT-SIZE: 10px;")
txtstream.WriteLine("    text-align: left;")
txtstream.WriteLine("    white-Space: nowrap;")
txtstream.WriteLine("    width: 100%;")
txtstream.WriteLine("}")
txtstream.WriteLine("select")
```

```
txtstream.WriteLine("{")
txtstream.WriteLine("    BORDER-RIGHT: #999999 3px solid;")
txtstream.WriteLine("    PADDING-RIGHT: 6px;")
txtstream.WriteLine("    PADDING-LEFT: 6px;")
txtstream.WriteLine("    FONT-WEIGHT: Normal;")
txtstream.WriteLine("    PADDING-BOTTOM: 6px;")
txtstream.WriteLine("    COLOR: white;")
txtstream.WriteLine("    PADDING-TOP: 6px;")
txtstream.WriteLine("    BORDER-BOTTOM: #999 1px solid;")
txtstream.WriteLine("    BACKGROUND-COLOR: navy;")
txtstream.WriteLine("    FONT-FAMILY: font-family: Cambria, serif;")
txtstream.WriteLine("    FONT-SIZE: 10px;")
txtstream.WriteLine("    text-align: left;")
txtstream.WriteLine("    white-Space: nowrap;")
txtstream.WriteLine("    width: 100%;")
txtstream.WriteLine("}")
txtstream.WriteLine("input")
txtstream.WriteLine("{")
txtstream.WriteLine("    BORDER-RIGHT: #999999 3px solid;")
txtstream.WriteLine("    PADDING-RIGHT: 3px;")
txtstream.WriteLine("    PADDING-LEFT: 3px;")
txtstream.WriteLine("    FONT-WEIGHT: Bold;")
txtstream.WriteLine("    PADDING-BOTTOM: 3px;")
txtstream.WriteLine("    COLOR: white;")
txtstream.WriteLine("    PADDING-TOP: 3px;")
txtstream.WriteLine("    BORDER-BOTTOM: #999 1px solid;")
txtstream.WriteLine("    BACKGROUND-COLOR: navy;")
txtstream.WriteLine("    FONT-FAMILY: font-family: Cambria, serif;")
txtstream.WriteLine("    FONT-SIZE: 12px;")
txtstream.WriteLine("    text-align: left;")
txtstream.WriteLine("    display: table-cell;")
txtstream.WriteLine("    white-Space: nowrap;")
txtstream.WriteLine("    width: 100%;")
```

```
txtstream.WriteLine("}")
txtstream.WriteLine("h1 {")
txtstream.WriteLine("color: antiquewhite;")
txtstream.WriteLine("text-shadow: 1px 1px 1px black;")
txtstream.WriteLine("padding: 3px;")
txtstream.WriteLine("text-align: center;")
txtstream.WriteLine("box-shadow: inset 2px 2px 5px rgba(0,0,0,0.5), inset -2px -2px 5px rgba(255,255,255,0.5)")
txtstream.WriteLine("}")
txtstream.WriteLine("</style>")
```

www.ingramcontent.com/pod-product-compliance
Lightning Source LLC
LaVergne TN
LVHW041216050326
832903LV00021B/656